THE HUMAN ARCH

Peter Cornwell was born in 1934, the son of an Anglican vicar, in Brislington on the outskirts of Bristol. He read theology at Worcester College, Oxford, completing his preparation for ordination at Cuddesdon Theological College. He was ordained to the diaconate of the Church of England in 1959 and to the priesthood the following year by the Archbishop of York, Michael Ramsey. After a curacy in Hull he returned to Cuddesdon, first as chaplain and later as Vice-Principal. In 1967 he became vicar of Silksworth, Co. Durham, in 1972 vicar of Barnard Castle, then in 1975 vicar of the University Church of St Mary the Virgin, Oxford. He resigned his living in May 1985 to become a member of the Roman Catholic Church and is now one of the small number of married Catholic priests in the UK. He works as a prison chaplain in Oxford.

PETER CORNWELL

THE HUMAN
ARCH

COLLINS
FOUNT PAPERBACKS

First published in Great Britain by Fount Paperbacks in 1990

Fount Paperbacks is an imprint of the Collins Publishing Group,
8 Grafton Street, London W1X 3LA

Typeset by Avocet Robinson, Buckingham
Printed and bound in Great Britain
by William Collins Sons & Co. Ltd, Glasgow

CONTENTS

INTRODUCTION

THE HUMAN ARCH –
A NEW GUIDING IMAGE?

What is an arch?

An arch is nothing else than a strength caused by two weaknesses; for the arch in buildings is made up of two segments of a circle, and each of these segments being in itself very weak desires to fall, and as one withstands the downfall of the other the two weaknesses are converted into a single strength. [1]

I have a personal reason for treasuring Leonardo da Vinci's definition of an arch. On the eve of our wedding, my wife sent it to me. For her it summed up the meaning of marriage. The two of us, in our incompleteness, were to be formed into a human arch, through our very weaknesses able to withstand the downfall of the other and so to find weakness converted into a single strength.

Reflecting on this image I have come to see that it is applicable to more than marriage. To be a complete fulfilled person is to live in a relationship of interdependence, of mutual support. Such interdependence is not the same as either dependence or independence. We all start life as totally dependent creatures. Indeed the human young seem to be more dependent and for longer than the young of any other species. So our first struggle is to grow out of this immature dependence to achieve a separate identity. Chips off the old block we may be, but we are not merely an extension of our parents. With a good deal of pain we have become our own people. But then there is something beyond such independence. As free mature persons we seek to give ourselves into a relationship of interdependence where we no longer stand on our own feet but learn to give and receive love in the human arch.

In what follows I shall be exploring the relevance of this image in our society. All societies live by bold images of what are held out to be the desirable life. As advertisers know, such images which grip the imagination are more effective than the small print of pedantic description. It is not otherwise in the sphere of religion, ethics or politics. Where dogma, fine reasoning and manifestos fail to reach, bold pictures can often go. This, of course, is not to denigrate critical reason, but simply to admit that reason has always to work on pictures, sometimes explicating them, sometimes criticising and taming them.

The dominating social images of recent years have been those of "independence". We have been encouraged to "be ourselves", "do our own thing", to make our own way unfettered by stultifying traditions and inhibiting conventions. "Do it yourself" has been the cry. Instead of calling in the plumber or electrician, we shall have a go at it ourselves. Instead of calling in religion or some other well-trod ethical path, we shall have a go at making up our own values. The picture which to my mind encapsulates this view of the desirable life is that of the shopper with trolley wending her way through a well-stocked supermarket plucking from the shelves whatever catches her fancy. The good life means being free to choose what you want.

This image of permitting or indeed encouraging the individual to make his or her own way has been associated in the public mind with the "permissive sixties". The conventional self-image of the eighties is that it is in revolt against the sixties. Certainly there have been "conservative" noises about a return to Victorian values, yet the predominant image fostered by the same Conservative leaders has in fact been a reinforcement of sixties independence. The foe has been not "do it yourself" but the allowing it to be done for you of the fifties dependency culture. Individuals are encouraged to stir their stumps, mount the ladder and use gifts and abilities to reach the starry heights of success. However much some places to which these ladders may carry aspirants may be deplored, the ladder image has remained in place.

The agument of this book is that this image of individual effort and independence is beginning to look worn and inadequate. It has not only lost its radical edge, but seems no longer to reflect the aspirations of the British public. We are a society in search of a new guiding image. I offer the image of the Human Arch as such. It speaks of something which does not deny the values of independence but points beyond them to the goal of interdependence. In chapter one I attempt an interpretation of the present situation in British society. In chapter two I offer reasons why Christians may be thought to have something useful to say on this matter of social goals while in chapters three and four I try to articulate how the movement from dependence to independence and then beyond to interdependence is quite fundamental to the way Christians believe and think. This vision of humanity as existing in a state of interdependence is no marginal "social" extra to basic faith, it is part and parcel of the praying, worshipping believing heart of it all. This means that the tiresome contemporary debate within the Church between "social gospel" and "traditional faith" is really quite redundant. Traditional faith is social gospel.

The fifth chapter tries to underline this point by an exposition of the teaching of Pope John Paul II in which social concern flows freely and naturally from the very centre of the gospel. As a Roman Catholic it is natural for me to use the Pope's teaching as an illustration of the coherence of the Christian vision. Other Christians will be able to show how their own particular traditions explicate similar coherence. If this vision of human interdependence is not marginal but central to Christian faith, we have then to confront the problem as to how Christians in a minority situation can be effective and get their message across. So the final chapters wrestle with the problem of religion which has become marginalized and privatized, just one can of beans on offer in the supermarket, and so how in our inescapably pluralist society it can step out of the ghetto into the market-place to contribute to the fashioning of a new guiding image of the common good without losing its identity and becoming a thinly disguised version of secularism.

This I take to be the crux of the matter. Does a pluralist society mean that any coherent notion of "society" or of the "common good" is dead? Must we stop talking about shared values and beliefs leaving each individual the lonely task of pursuing his or her personal goal? Is the only common goal the fashioning of a framework which will give us maximum freedom to pursue our private goals? Here I believe lies the great divide and I have no doubt on which side of that divide orthodox traditional faith lies. It has always located individual freedom and flourishing within the giving and receiving of a common life. Of course I do not pretend that Christians are the only believers in this goal of "the common good". Many of other faiths and of no faith are potential allies in this task of reconstruction. Christians are in no position to head a triumphalist return to the common life of Christendom. Neither do I pretend that it will be easy to identify a good which is really common, values which in fact we share. My hunch is that we shall not be able to do much more than edge forward in an Abraham-like way searching for the good of the city which is to come. But on one thing we shall be clear: pluralism is not enough. We must begin together to construct a common life or perish.

The main theme of this book is the search for an image of this common life, a picture which will capture the imagination because it connects with aspirations which the supermarket image has left untouched. In this sense I am more concerned with a social goal rather than the paths to that goal, with ends rather than means, with a vision rather than with politics. However I shall skate on very thin ice and get perilously near to politics. Many will judge that I have gone through the ice and the cry will go up once more: "What is a priest doing meddling in politics?" I have to say that I have few sleepless nights worrying about whether I am being "too political". After all politics are just to do with practical ways of trying to effect social goals, measures taken in the human city to translate theory into practice. Because I can see no merit in simply dreaming dreams in the wilderness, I am all for politics. As a priest I can pretend to no divine guaranteed wisdom. I hand out no political manifesto inscribed in tablets of stone by the finger of God. Indeed my faith tells me that between the final guiding vision of the Kingdom of God and our stumbling attempts to move just a few paces towards it, there is a great and permanent gulf fixed. My faith warns me off the idolatry of politics, off trying to turn political parties and programmes into little gods. But my faith does not thereby encourage me to be apolitical, piously floating above what the fastidious call "the dirty world of politics". Ways and means may not be gods but they are necessary servants. In this, as St. James so pithily puts it, we are to be "doers of the word, and not hearers only" (James 1:22).

The prejudice of course remains that religion is to do with something called "the spiritual side of life". Mrs Thatcher in her famous speech to the General Assembly of the Church of Scotland expounded, not for the first time, this division of labour. Christianity, she declared is "about spiritual redemption, not social reform". Let religion with its professional practitioners stick to the spiritual side of life which would include sharpening up private morality and leave politicians to deal with public life. My problem is that I find it genuinely difficult to understand how in Christian terms this "carve up" can be justified. I suppose it is based on the common misreading of Christ's words: "Render to Caesar the things that are Caesar's, and to God the things that are God's" (see Mark 12:13–17) and on a Lutheran tradition of the Two Realms. The gospel saying, with the implicit contrast between a coin, a dead thing, stamped with the image of the emperor and man stamped with the image and likeness of God, contains a rather more explosive punch than has been thought. Far from dividing the human realm between God and Caesar, the Lord seems to say: "Let Caesar keep his coins. People belong to God." As for any hermetically sealed doctrine of two realms, with Church and state keeping their distance, that surely died the death in Nazi Germany in the thirties, as the Confessing Church opposed the practical capitulation of the German Christians to the state.

The simple truth is that the faith of Holy Scripture knows no such dualism. For the Bible there is no "spiritual side" of life. All real life which is inescapably physical and therefore social and political is yet spiritual. Take the story of the prophet Elijah on Mount Horeb (1 Kings 19). It is one of sublime spirituality – the unveiling of the mystery of God in the "still small voice", and yet it is also a tale of politics, of the prophet commissioned by God to anoint rival leaders, Hazael and Jehu who will effect a coup and depose the corrupt and unjust Ahab. Or turn to the Book of Amos:

> Hear this you who trample the needy, and bring the poor
> of the land to an end, saying "When will the new moon
> be over, that we may sell grain?
> And the Sabbath, that we may offer wheat for sale,
> that we may make the ephah small and the shekel great,
> and deal deceitfully with false balances,
> that we may buy the poor for silver
> and the needy for a pair of sandals,
> and sell the refuse of the wheat?" (Amos 8:4–6)

Is that all about the "spiritual side" of life? Is it not also about the victims of market forces? In fact is not the spirituality of it precisely the discernment of the involvement of God in these secular matters? "Surely", says God, "I will never forget any of their deeds" (verse 7.)

Any dualism between politics and prayer is overcome by the dogmatic heart of faith, the incarnation of the eternal Son of God. Because God speaks out of the silence of his mystery and that word is made flesh, flesh, this world of materiality and political arrangement, is shown in all its potential. Such earthen vessels can become carriers of the life of the kingdom. The Christian task, as revealed in our central act of worship, the Eucharist, is to affirm the God-carrying potential of the material, to insist that the mystery of God cannot be shunted into the sidelines of some specialist spiritual hobby but lays claim to every department of life. To believe any less would be to acquiesce in a practical polytheism, with separate gods to run religion, politics and the market. Jesus says "No servant can serve two masters. . . . You cannot serve God and money" (Luke 16:13).

So I shall skate on thin ice without apology. I would rather I got my feet a little wet with political dabbling, than give the suggestion that faith is for dreaming when we tire of the real world. I would rather chance my arm with a few very fallible political pointers than wholly disappear in a cloud of beautiful theory. Christians will part company with Karl Marx at a number of points, but in this at least they claim together a common hebraic heritage, over the essential practicalness of their theory. In the famous words of the eleventh Thesis against Feuerbach: "The Philosophers have only interpreted the world in various ways; the point, however, is to change it." Which after all is very close to our Lord's description of the wise man who builds his house on rock – the one who "hears these words of mine and does them" (Matthew 7:24). What are politics but the inhabitants of human city acting together for the common good, taking a few faltering steps to allow the word of the vision to be made flesh?

Note

1. Leonardo da Vinci, *Selections from the Notebooks,* World's Classics
    edition, p. 210.

ONE

THE ROTTING LADDER –
LOOKING BEYOND
INDIVIDUALISM

The ladder to freedom

"A policy of freedom for the individual is the only truly progressive policy."[1] This claim sums up F.A. Hayek's influential tract against socialism. In it the author rejects state intervention and central planning and renews the call of nineteenth-century liberalism to individual responsibility and initiative. The state has a role but it is a modest one, that of providing a framework within which various activities can be conducted by different persons according to their individual plans. The state would confine itself "to creating conditions under which the knowledge and initiative of individuals is given the best scope so *they* can plan most successfully".[2]

Hayek's *Road to Serfdom* has some claim to be the Bible of the new conservatism for the aim and object of this recent trend in British politics has been to roll back the frontiers of an ever more intrusive state, to abandon central planning and release the energies of individuals. Despite the fact that this aim has paradoxically been accompanied by great increases in state power, notably in the fields of local government and education, the programme of privatization of state corporations and council housing has been enthusiastically followed through. Greater opportunity has been given to individuals and some attempt made to eliminate what was felt to be an unhealthy dependence on state welfare. Although a welfare safety net has been retained, people are increasingly encouraged to turn away from it and launch out to become high-flyers. Personal responsibility for our own lives and the exercise of personal obligation towards our own dependents, has become the goal.

The political success of the new conservatism is shown in the way it has been able to thrust aside the title "conservative" and appear as a truly radical and innovative force in society. It has won considerable popular support, particularly amongst the striving and successful, but also amongst those who have newly become owners of homes and shares. It has often made its opponents on the left appear like backward-looking conservationists. In response the left has seemed content to gnash its collective teeth in an ideological wilderness or to mourn the "good old days" of the Butskellite pale pinkish consensus of the immediate post-war years. While it will become clear that I see considerable merit in that consensus and indeed believe that the future for a united nation must lie in some development of it, I fully recognize that there can be no nostalgic return to the past. The word "development" is crucial. If there are signs that the new individualist liberalism is already wearing thin, we must not be deceived into imagining that the clock can be simply put back to the fifties and sixties. The future belongs to those who have taken the measure of the appeal of "Thatcherism" and had the courage to take on board some of its insights.

In search of the right road

I have already said that I hope that I will not stray too far into the realm of politics though I admit that I shall find this difficult. After all politics is simply to do with the affairs of the city, the practical measures which are inescapably necessary if one wants to move society in a particular direction. However I want to make it clear that the intention of this book is to be concerned with the vision of what our society ought to be, the direction in which we ought to go. I hold this to be a valid exercise and indeed would judge that one of the weaknesses of the post-war consensus was that as it plodded on it gradually lost any very clear idea of where it wanted to go. If idealism without practicality is not enough, neither is pragmatism without principle. If as Britons we are usually content to exercise our gift for "sustained practical activity", keeping on the march, R.H. Tawney recognized that there are times "which are not ordinary, and in such times it is not enough to follow the road. It is necessary to know where it leads and, if it leads nowhere, to follow another. . . . the practical thing for the traveller who is uncertain of his path is not to proceed with the utmost rapidity in the wrong direction; it is to consider how to find the right one."[3]

While Mrs Thatcher would disagree profoundly with Tawney's understanding of which is the right path, she would fully agree that you cannot work out how to get somewhere without first establishing where you want to go. She is a conviction politician, impatient of fudge and mudge, scornful of a patched-up consensus, with a burning zeal to propagate a vision of society which is set against what she believes to be the political orthodoxy of the sixties. She knows where she is going. Because the electorate is more interested in the general direction than the small print of party political programmes, such purposefulness seems to be part of her appeal.

The competing strands of conservatism

Yet in the very clarity of her vision there may lie dangers. Not only has the Prime Minister announced her desire to wipe socialism off the political map of Great Britain, but she has also bid fair to destroy one strand of her own party's tradition, that of the "one nation" school whose roots are in the countryside and which has been as critical of urban liberal economics as it has been of state socialism. In fact this strand of the party can lay greater claim to the title "Conservative" than its economically liberal bedfellows. Here is a tradition which believes in a coherent national life, a belonging together and interdependence which produce the fruit of common values and beliefs. It stirs uneasily when assaults are made on local government, when the independence and academic excellence of universities seem threatened, when free enterprise bids to dismantle laws designed for the protection of the environment or the national architectural heritage. With its concern for the quality of life, it is a strange partner for unbridled *laissez-faire,* "every man for himself" capitalism. If there are murmurs of dissatisfaction with the current orthodoxy of Hayek individualism, they come as much from within the Conservative Party as from outside. Indeed it is arguable that the most effective opposition to government policies has come from Conservatives of this school in the House of Lords.

Such is the clarity of Mrs Thatcher's vision and such has been her impatience with dissent within the ranks that she may have overlooked the fact that her party, like any other, has in the end to operate as a "Broad Church", able to contain a good deal of diversity. Conservatives have been less indulgent about putting such diversity on public view than their rivals on the left for whom life would not be the same without a good conference "punch-up", yet in truth their party is as much a coalition as any other. Broad Churches and coalitions are not the happiest hunting grounds for leaders with clear dogmatic teaching and sharp visions.

My argument is that the individualism of economic liberalism which has recently reigned supreme is an insufficient vision for society, and that the stirrings against the dominance of market forces as the measure of all things can be discerned not only on the left but within the traditional right as well. Things move on in politics, and what may once have seemed the bright radical hope for the day may look distinctly outmoded only a few years later. Conservatives of the new breed may be in danger of doing what, with some justice, they have accused their opponents on the left or in the middle of doing, settling down in party dogma and failing to persist in the continuing task of critical thinking.

Learning the lessons of Thatcherism

But, if we are to move onwards, we can only do so having absorbed the lessons which Thatcherism has taught us. It achieved political success because it rang bells with national sentiments which lay buried beneath the genial consensus of the sixties. The British have never been enamoured of centralism with its large corporations, whether publicly or privately owned. Indeed the question of who owns what has stirred few hearts and it has been largely seen as one to be answered in a pragmatic rather than dogmatic way. While many can see the point of making accumulations of power responsible and of withdrawing certain necessities of life, like health and education, from the market-place, few can see the virtue in either dogmatic nationalization or dogmatic privatization. What is disliked anywhere is faceless bureaucracy which prevents the employee or consumer from getting at the person in charge. That is felt to be as objectionable in a private monopoly as in a public one. We have met it in our dealings with the local council, the government department and in a privatized British Telecom. We dislike being diminished by the council official or the bland secretary which the large firm has put in place to field our complaints. We do not take to being pushed around, especially when the pusher deems that it is for our own good. If the blood goes to our head when we are confronted by the scarcely polite evasion of the company agent to whom we have made some complaint, it goes rather more to our head when some high-minded social worker uses the power of charity to strip us of all dignity.

On the contrary, life feels good when we know that our economic power is recognized, when we are treated as the honoured consumer on whom the producer and salesman depend. Even if it is only because it has been perceived that courtesy and good service form the path to profit, it is nonetheless welcome and from whatever quarter it comes. Being treated as the customer who knows best, as an individual who is valued, is worth more to us than the knowledge that the firm is either publicly or privately owned. We are all individualists at least in this respect that we want to be treated as individuals.

This means as well that we are radical libertarians. We covet the freedom to be fulfilled by fostering our own gifts and making our own way. We do not accept that the development of our little field of excellence should be held back from fear that others might feel envious and disadvantaged. Of course if Jack's flourishing is at the expense of Jill's diminishment, if his freedom robs her of freedom, then that is another matter, for we recognize that the reverse side of this coin of freedom is our personal responsibility. Indeed to be free to flourish means also that we ask to be treated as responsible human beings, and therefore not allowed like elephants to dance uninhibitedly while chickens are around.

I once lived in a part of the North East which desperately needed opportunities for such individual initiative and flourishing. It was an area rich in community skills but poor in the sort of excellence which would raise expectations. Poverty and insecurity of many years' standing had bred too much acceptance of the third-rate, so that people were, in a way too contented. For the quality of our common life we desperately needed pace-setters, those who would raise our sights to see that far more was achievable than we had dared to imagine, who would show that we did not need hand-outs from remote government in London, that we could do things ourselves and so enhance our dignity and self-respect. So it was sad to see doctrinaire educational policies destroying here an established grammar school, there a direct grant school, both of which had been proven providers of the very qualities we needed. Of course it was all well-intentioned, done to enhance the equal value of persons and thus to enhance the common life, and yet what we missed was the perception that this common life needed to be served by individual giftedness. The theory that such freedom to flourish would continue in the new comprehensive schools and that we could have the best of all worlds did not always work in practice. Good educational communities, like any other communities, take time to grow. When you have one which delivers the goods it is perilous to tear it down in pursuit of some ideology. For all your good intentions the result may be not the enhancement but the diminishment of the common life.

In so far as we are now able uninhibitedly to celebrate individual freedom and achievement, in so far as we cease to treat passing the buck of responsibility onto "Them" as the natural reaction to all difficulties, in so far as society is enriched by the pursuit of excellence, we can be grateful for the Thatcherite revolution. Values have been affirmed which needed affirming. If we are to advance beyond this revolution, we must do justice to its strong points. But advance we surely must. The record cannot be allowed to get stuck in the groove of an economic liberalism which is already displaying fundamental problems.

Problems of the new conservatism – a failure in distribution

The first of such problems concerns the uneven distribution of the benefits of individual freedom. If, in George Orwell's *Animal Farm*, some animals in this totalitarian utopia turned out to be more equal than others, in the Britain of the eighties some are certainly more free than others. It is not the case that the less free are only slowly catching up with the more free, but that the divide between those to whom ever more choices are open and those to whom choices are ever more restricted is a growing divide. Behind the rhetoric of individual freedom lies the inescapable fact of power, and behind that fact lies the equally inescapable fact of money. As long as we interpret freedom as the ability to choose between a range of services and goods, it is clear that in this world at least the extent of choice is determined by wealth. The more money we have, the more freedom of this sort we have.

The opportunity and initiative state has proved good for some and less good for others. As the state has taken less in direct taxation, the "haves" are favoured and so the gap between rich and poor has increased. The theory is, of course, that the poor are, in the end, assisted by the enrichment of the rich, through what has come to known as the "trickle down" effect. As top persons get wealthier they demand ever more goods and services and this, so the argument runs, creates new jobs and thus ultimately greater affluence for all. The theory works imperfectly, as the growing demand turns out to be for Japanese hi-fi equipment and French wine. Even when the theory can be shown to work, it works slowly and in the meantime causes strain and resentment within society. The benefits of initiative and enterprise are celebrated in the face of those who have not the jobs in which to reveal these qualities. Hour by hour television commercials dangle before the poor styles of life which are totally out of their reach. In the old days the poor could at least keep away from those areas where their poverty was mocked by the ostentatious displays of wealth, but now it relentlessly invades their homes. Life seems unfair. While there are tax-cuts for the rich, the less well off have their housing benefit cut in order to assist those who are even less well off than they are. While it is deemed necessary to attract the successful with the glittering prizes of ever greater salaries, a different motivation is deployed for those at the bottom of the pile; they must be taught not to "price themselves out of the market", to be content with lower wages under threat of unemployment, from which castrated trade unions can no longer save them.

It is carrot for the successful and stick for the unsuccessful. In our locality there was recently a refuse collectors' strike. Our cheerful and courteous dustmen had worked hard, with the result that it was concluded that they could do their work in less time and at less cost to the ratepayers. Industry was to be rewarded by a cut in the working week and in wages. No wonder a union banner carried the complaint: "Let's all work harder to become poor faster."

The heady slogan "free choice" masks realities which are more sobering. It is attractive to claim that the sick should be able to choose the time when they can be admitted into hospital, but the truth is that such choice is limited to those who can afford private health insurance schemes. It sounds good to say that parents should be able to choose what sort of school their children should attend, that if they are dissatisfied with what is provided by the local authority, they should have the freedom to withdraw their children's school from that authority. Yet again the appearance of freedom is deceptive. The freedom to opt out may be exercised by parents say in 1990, yet it cannot be exercised by a subsequent set of new parents in 1994. Nobody grumbles about the acquisition of freedom. It is a commodity we cannot have enough of. Yet what is on offer is often the freedom to walk around a plentifully stocked supermarket with an abundance of goods. "Put in your trolley, whatever you want!" Who could resist such an invitation? And yet there is a snag. Each one of us still has our moment of truth at the cash desk. There the embarrassment begins, for there we shall only be free to have what we can pay for.

The libertarian right would reject such "moralising" on the results of market forces. People are poor, it is argued, either because they have chosen a way of life like vagrancy which involves poverty or because of "misfortune". The mechanism of the market is impersonal. It does not intend to make people poor. The language of moral praise or blame is thus inappropriate to the results of its workings. It seems to me doubtful that the market can be treated in this way as a sort of mysterious fate, even as a god. Moreover moral responsibility extends considerably further than areas covered by conscious "intentions". It is notorious that the way to Hell is paved with good intentions. The driver speeding through a built-up area does not intend to hurt a fly. Nevertheless he may still maim and kill – and he will rightly be counted responsible for what he does. If there are victims as well as winners of "market forces", we cannot praise the God Mammon for the latter, and cry "There is no one really to blame" for the former.

Problems of the new conservatism – libertarianism or common values

The second problem is a contradiction inherent in the new conservatism. Is the freedom for which we aim simply to be a freedom to do what each individual wants? Within the new right there are consistent libertarians who, while allowing the state to hold the ring and prevent me from using my freedom to the detriment of my neighbour's freedom, believe that values and morals are not for state promotion. We ought to accept the free market in the sphere of values and beliefs. No paternalist authority, whether it be Church or state, should be telling me what I ought to do. If I wish to endanger my health with drugs, drink or smoking, I should be free to do so. As long as I do not impinge on the freedom of others, I should be able to follow my own path. Such consistent libertarians are understandably sceptical of talk about "common values and beliefs", and tend to see "nationality" as nothing more that the provision of an umbrella of law and order under which individuals should be free to do their own thing. Even Mrs

Thatcher has said that she does not believe in an entity called "society".

Such a position seems the logical outworking of the new conservatism yet it is clearly at odds with the older "one nation" school and the current reaction to the libertarianism of the permissive sixties. The very party which has called the nation to individual liberties finds itself pressed to call for a return to old *common* values and beliefs. In this it is responsive to a growing sense of unease with deviant patterns of behaviour and to an instinctive belief that society needs the glue of some agreed values to hold it together. Everyone for himself seems not quite enough. When video nasties were shown in the Palace of Westminster, Members of Parliament were revolted. Instead of arguing that, while such things did not appeal to them personally they might appeal to others, they came out determined to act for the common good and try to draw limits. The state had a task more positive than that of simply holding the ring for individuals to be free to fashion their own ways of life; there was a thing called "the common good", the state had to have some care for the way of life of a whole people. This of course was not merely a matter of the creation of laws, although such laws were sometimes required.

Indeed it has also been perceived that the observance of law requires something more than the force of law to sustain it. Behind effective law enforcement there has to lie a general acceptance by society that such laws are just and good. Positive law, the rule of some authority which says "Do this – Don't do that", only works where the injunction is felt to reflect values to which the majority assents, at least in its better moments. This was clearly seen in a House of Lords debate on violence in society. The then Lord Chancellor argued that the violence of criminals was but the tip of an iceberg, that the mugger and armed robber were extreme examples of a society in which turning to violence had insidiously become more acceptable. The violence which hits the headlines should be seen as a sinister sacrament of a society which is less convinced that violence is wrong and more ready to turn to it when desires are frustrated. In this perception there is an implicit rejection of consistent libertarianism and a recognition of the need for common values and beliefs.

T.S. Eliot was one of the great articulators of this traditional Conservative belief in the need for such a coherent national way of life. He condemned the liberal-secular society as a vacuum which would be impossible to sustain. Such a room, swept and garnished, would not remain for ever empty. Unless filled with good positive values, it would be invaded by the demons of totalitarian ideologies. The libertarian society, he held, was unsustainable. In his own day he perceived marxism and fascism moving in to fill the jaded emptiness of a post-Christian society. However while Eliot was critical of cultural liberal individualism, he seemed blind to the economic liberalism which undergirded that British class system to which he was somewhat sentimentally attached. As Raymond Williams pointed out, Eliot was trying to lay a strong view of the common life on top of an essentially divisive, "every man for himself" economic substructure. Although economic structures do not create values, neither do values float free above such mundane realities.

We are perhaps beginning to see this increasingly clearly in our society. Anyone who takes seriously the gulf between inner city and outer suburb, between the North East and the South East, anyone who has crossed the divide between leafy lanes with spacious housing to the wastelands of graffiti-adorned high-rise flats and decaying shopping areas, knows that he is moving out of one world into another. How realistic is it to speak of values common to both worlds, of a shared way of life, indeed of one nation? The new conservatism seems so far to have failed to reconcile its economic liberalism and individualism with that ever more apparent need to refashion a sense of common purpose and identity. Mrs Thatcher herself seems torn between the two conservatisms. Denying the existence of "society" she stands with the libertarians; calling for a return to "Victorian values" she is with those who seek some form of a common life.

Problems of the New Conservatism – the loss of the common life

This contradiction within conservatism brings us to its third problem, its failure to do justice to the "common life" as a value in its own right. It is not simply that human beings need glue to prevent society from lapsing into the sort of anarchy which would imperil our personal liberties, it is that we hold "belonging together" as a separate and distinct good. If I need to be myself, I need also to relate to others. While deliberately chosen solitariness is good for a while, we fear loneliness which is imposed on us. If our neighbours become a source of threat, if we sit huddled in the home for fear of walking the streets, then we are not enjoying proper privacy but are imprisoned in loneliness. The awfulness of violence in our streets is that it deprives us of a freedom to be amongst others. If I need to be myself, my own person, I equally need to relate to others.

This of course takes place at different levels of intensity. At its deepest we find it amongst family and friends but we also need it in a less intense way, at the level of "nodding acquaintance", to be able to exchange a few words with the shop assistant, to pass the time of day in the street, to have a joke with the postman. These levels of human relations help us to feel at home in the world, to discover it as friendly and not hostile, and so help us to move with greater ease. One of our present troubles may be that these real, although less intense, relationships have broken down, life has become more impersonal, and so we are increasingly driven in on fewer but more intense relationships. The breakdown of these latter relationships may in part be due to the fact that too much strain is imposed on them as they fail to open out into these other wider but less intense relationships.

Let me give some examples of where we experience the benefit of this level of sociability. It happens that I do not drive a car. This has many disadvantages in terms of mobility, but it does mean that I can discover some of the advantages of public transport. Instead of being sealed up in my private vehicle, I can appreciate the particular flavour of the common life of bus travel. There is the back-chat between the driver and his regular passengers. There are fascinating snippets of conversation to be overheard about onions and bunions. Despite its frequent inconvenience, I find that travelling on a bus offers me a particular level of social life which helps me to feel happy and at home in the world. I constantly find myself thinking "How kindly and decent most people really are."

It is the same with the old "corner shop" or village stores. Of course the supermarket will offer you a wider, and indeed cheaper, range of goods. Just as the private car wins every time in terms of the simple task of transportation, so the supermarket is the more efficient selling machine. But then I am something more than a dedicated buyer and as something more I have to say that I find the supermarket depressingly impersonal. You dash around with your trolley, snatching at this and that, and end up having your acquisitions priced by a glazed-eye girl at the cash desk who seems in a state of perpetual trance. The corner shop or the village stores is an altogether warmer and more humane place. Here you get more than you came into the shop for, fascinating gossip, hot local news and the opportunity for a little conversation. It is here that that illusive commodity, "community" is forged.

For six years we lived in a mining village. The fact that there was a population of some twelve thousand in no way diminished the reality of "villageness". Ours was a real community. Down in the pit work could not be done on the principle of "every man for himself", the task required team-work and interdependence. Here in human solidarity the community's sense of identity was born. Yet it extended beyond the pit into our village streets. The colliery had known hard times, high unemployment and real poverty, and in such times survival depended on trust and mutual help. Although we lived there during a time of relative affluence, we could see how this spirit of neighbourliness endured. Do not get me wrong. This was no Garden of Eden. There was as much human failure and frailty as anywhere else, but the obligation to help one another was recognized as a common value, it was accepted as a requirement of true human living. By and large it worked. Old people were not left to die in loneliness and cold; they were treated as valued members of the community with a continuing role to play, whether as child-minders or dispensers of, sometimes rather dubious, conventional wisdom to their married daughters. No bereaved person was left to the cruel privacy of their grief. Where there was need, neighbours felt that it was not only right, but natural, to move in to help.

This was not simply a "crisis" commodity. A sense of solidarity could be felt in our somewhat grotty streets. Here it was natural to pass the time of day with everyone you met and to chat with all and sundry as you went about your business. The remarkable thing was that something quite familiar in the old rural villages was able to extend to such a large population. If we are really to talk comprehensively about freedom, we must surely include this freedom to feel that you "belong", that this place is your home. Of course we must not be sentimental. There are times when we value the anonymity of the impersonal city, that other freedom to be in the crowd and yet not intruded on. The warm community can squash us in its embrace, be a tyrannical parent which extracts conformism in exchange for protectiveness. Such communities with their strong ties and common values can be inimicable to individual initiative and personal fulfilment. The young can be inhibited by the community's expectations from spreading their wings, breaking out of the mould and fulfilling their potential. I have known too many school leavers held back from aspiring to higher education to be blind to the genial but iron tyranny of such communities.

Without denying in any way that there can be conflict with individual liberty, I want to claim that here is a particular good, that of sociability or belonging, which in fact people value. It is something many want to be free to enjoy. It is by now notorious that the unemployed have had set before them the initiative of one who got on his bicycle to leave home in search of a job. The message is: "If you want to get on, you must get out." The market indeed requires that men should move where their labour is required. And yet the cost must be counted. The way of mobility is the way of death for many communities, the destruction of patterns of life and common values which have been forged over the years. How do you weigh in the balance the good of economic efficiency and the good of such communities? Must the market be the measure of all things?

When a neighbouring colliery closed, the National Coal Board took great trouble not only in the careful running down of the pit, but in offering new jobs and homes to redundant miners down south in the coal fields near Stoke on Trent. Nobody had to get on any bike. It was all laid on. A handful made the trek and stayed, most would not even consider it. Some went and were back within a few weeks. What was wrong? Simply that the Staffordshire collieries were not home, not the place where they belonged. Life meant more than having a job, it meant sharing a community way of life, belonging to this working men's club, exercising one's whippets, racing one's pigeons, caring for one's allotment. Here was a very particular pattern of life, a niche which one valued. This common life on the dole was considered better than to be uprooted and to make a new life with employment.[4]

It is easy for the comfortable middle classes to write this

off as self-indulgent nostalgia. At the time of the Miners'
Strike, I recall an Oxford don who, from the security of life
tenure of a college fellowship which he had held for many
years, berated the immobility of the miners. "The days of
coal are over. They need to face the facts and go in search
of new work. A change is good for us all!"

What is at stake here is not only a freedom to share in
a particular way of life, but the future of the very
communities which are proven carriers of common values
and beliefs. It is simply no good politicians waking up to
the need for the glue of such values and beliefs and shouting
that we ought to have them. Some reflection is required on
how values and beliefs are fostered and disseminated. There
is simply no doubt at all that such communities are the
effective communicators of values. We cannot have our cake
and eat it. We cannot one minute cry for the glue of common
values and the next carelessly throw to destruction the very
bodies which brew the glue. Once again we perceive the
contradiction of conservatism – a cry for a common life
combined with a fostering of economic liberalism which can
do nothing but destroy that common life.

Interdependence – not idealism but fact of human life

Here of course it is argued that we are simply pitting idealism
against the hard facts of the real world. Yet the claim of
the "common life" springs not from high-minded
conservation of some nostalgic dream but from an
observation of reality. The truth about human living is the
truth about interdependence. As John Finnis reminds us:
"there is physical, biological, ecological interdependence,
there is a vast common stock of knowledge, and there is
a vast common stock of technology, systems of inter-
communication, ideological symbolism, universal
religions".[5]

The facts of life show not solidarity and interdependence
but solitariness and independence to be the dream. In truth

31

we are all bound up together in the bundle of life. Popular scientific programmes on TV open our eyes to the subtle intricacies of the food chains on which animals depend. They show, too, man's dependence on the animal and inanimate order. Our eyes have been opened to a vision of man both more wonderful in its complexity and yet more humbling. If we have the ability to get to the moon yet we are really of the earth, earthy. In tune with this perception the Green Movement struggles to teach us a way of living which is not high-minded idealism but in accord with these facts of life.

Far from growing away from such interdependence through our technological skills, we are bound more and more closely to one another by them. The communications revolution makes it impossible for anyone to be an island. So Vatican Council II spoke not wild idealism but plain truth when it said: "Because of the closer bonds of human interdependence and their spread over the whole world, we are today witnessing a widening role of the common good." The conflict between this fact and the resurgence of economic liberalism was illustrated in 1987 when the money market, the very symbol of such liberalism, revealed that it could not float free from the chains of interdependence. The money market rocked as what happened in New York and Tokyo affected dealings in London. Collapse could only be averted by that sworn foe of economic liberalism, collective planning and joint action. Even more poignantly is this brought home by the economies of those Third World countries imprisoned in their struggle to service enormous debts. Increasingly their freedom to pursue policies which seem suitable for their societies is restricted by conditions laid down by the International Monetary Fund.

At the very moment when the rich world seems to be turning its back on collective action and notions of the "common good" in favour of individual enterprise, we are discovering that in dealing with the real world, its environment, its economy, the fate of its poor, such individualism is not enough. To talk about human beings as if they were lone independent units free to scrabble up private ladders to success and fulfilment is to talk about creatures which do not really exist. Yet we persist in doing so. Take one symptomatic example of how the language of illusory individualism leads us astray. In debates on abortion it is inescapably necessary to have a working definition of human life. One way of doing this has been to use the measuring rod of "viability". The foetus is accorded human status when it is "viable", capable of "independent" existence. But what is independent existence? A new-born baby is not capable of independent existence. It cannot look after itself. The classical world knew this and so when it wanted to get rid of unwanted babies, mainly female, they would be allowed to come to term and then be abandoned on the mountains. If to be human is to be independent and to be dependent is to be sub-human, the opportunities for ridding ourselves of inconvenient creatures is almost unlimited, not only the very young but also the very old and the disabled in the middle would have the dignity of humanity stripped from them and become eligible for the scrap heap. Indeed if independence is the measure of humanity, we have to ask at what point any of us is capable of such independent existence.

Reconciling liberty and equality in human solidarity

There are good reasons then for believing that Hayek's gospel of pure individualism and its propagation by the new conservatism is inadequate. Indeed adherence to it has generated a fresh call for common values which its political embodiment cannot produce. Individuals evidently treasure, not only the freedom to do their own thing, but also freedom to feel at home with other individuals, to enjoy the fruits of community, to lean on other people in the expectation that they too will lean on us. This is not surprising because the facts of life speak of such interdependence. It is the way we are made. The task set before us seems clear – to weld together those values we have rediscovered in the new conservatism, the freedom of individuals to flourish in their glorious variety, the dignity of being responsible, with our need for a truly common life with its commitment to common values. Liberty and equality need to be reconciled in fraternity/sorority, or human solidarity.

The task – political

This is of course partly a political task. Inescapably, we have to labour to produce policies, ways and means, of at least encouraging such a reconciliation. We cannot float above the flesh of politics. Although in the end programmes and policies may not create freedom and community, they can powerfully influence our movement in one direction or another, or at least check that movement. Certainly the new conservatism has not been lacking in belief in the effectiveness of political measures in promoting its own understanding of the "good life". We all know that centrist state policies can inhibit individual freedom and that *laissez-faire* economics can destroy resources of common life. While central planning seems to have inhibited individual initiative and responsibility in the Soviet Union, the rule of market forces has destroyed human communities in South Wales and the North East. Political arrangement is not everything, but it is something. Those who are concerned to fashion a world a bit more fit for free persons to live in solidarity cannot wash their hands of the nuts and bolts of these practical decisions and actions which may help or hinder their objectives.

The task – cultural

Yet, at the end of the day, the task is more fundamentally a cultural one, that is, one which concerns the whole way of life of a people, of the goals and beliefs which a society publicly honours and therefore sets before us. It is a question of conviction about the things which are held to be good for our human flourishing. While this must set the direction for political action, it is something more than that. It can become a conviction, a vision which those of different political parties share, leaving room for argument and disagreement about ways and means to embody this vision. To become a common goal, a shared vision, it has to be something more than a matter for leisured debate amongst academics, it has to be able to grip the imagination of a people and grip that imagination so successfully that it stirs us into action. In the post-war years, it could be said that a vision of the Welfare State thus captured the collective imagination. It was something generally agreed upon. And then mysteriously the vision faded and a new one took its place, that of the independent individualist standing on his own feet, liberated to use his talents and opportunities. What we are after now is a common vision which brings freedom and fellowship together, a vision powerful enough to both capture the imagination of our society and stir it into effective action.

Notes

1. F. A. Hayek, *The Road to Serfdom,* 1944, A&K edition, 1986, p. 178.
2. *Ibid.* p. 26.
3. R. H. Tawney, *The Acquisitive Society,* Fontana 1961. pp. 9–10.
4. See *Ryhope: A pit closes – a study in redeployment,* HMSO 1970.
5. John Finnis, *Natural Law and Natural Rights,* Clarendon Press 1980, p. 150.

TWO

SPEAKING FROM EXPERIENCE – THE CASE FOR A CHRISTIAN CONTRIBUTION

Why should anyone imagine that Christianity has anything to contribute to the forging of such a vision of society? Believers claim that in the living and dying of Jesus of Nazareth the vital clue is given not only to the question "Who or what is God?" but also to the question "What is it to be truly human?" Yet that claim is either denied or thought to be irrelevant to the particular social questions we have posed.

Two ways of privatizing faith

To many of our contemporaries the claims of faith seem about as probable as those of astrologers and alchemists. In a secular society they may be tolerated as the private foibles of a minority but are seen to possess no intrinsic authority. While it may be admitted that society needs aims and ideals, these, it is said, have to be forged by the reason and imagination of a human race which has no access to esoteric "divine" information. Let Christians, if they will, join us in the pursuit of wisdom, but, if they are to be useful, they must renounce appeals to some "higher" source of knowledge. Let them be content to join the human race in the humbler task of creating its own values.

To others who do believe the claims of faith, a particular "Christian" contribution to the construction of society is equally problematic. While there should be Christians involved as individuals in the affairs of state, there can be no "Christian" answers to its problems. Christ's Kingdom is a kingdom "not of this world". Between his Kingdom and those of this world a deep gulf lies. While every human city lies under the judgement of the City of God, the task of faith is "otherworldly" the forging of a union between God and the individual in prayer and sacrament and through this the fashioning of a personal morality. The fruits of such faith are highly honoured and indeed believed to be very relevant to the needs of society. Religion can do what no politician can do, teach a way of righteousness which encourages personal responsibility, proclaim high standards in domestic and business life, and thus, without daring into the technical specialized world of economics, commerce and power politics, help to create good citizens. A respectable and indeed honoured niche in society is thus accorded to Christianity, provided it plays the game and sticks to what is held to be its proper task.

These two views have at least this in common that both acquiesce in the privatization of religion. While to the first, belief is a mistaken though permissable eccentricity, to the second it is held to be true for the individual but not for society. Christians dissatisfied with this division of labour would be wise to recognize that the current dislike of social Christianity is not without reason. It can be a protest against a faith which seems to have lost confidence in its essential message. Because its word about "sin" and "redemption", God and prayer, worship and the pursuit of "holiness" ring few bells in a secular society, the Church, it is alleged, has turned in it frustration to areas where it believes it can be heard. Christianity, unsure of its gospel, busies itself with fascinating distractions. It becomes obsessed with internal matters such as church government, the ordination of women and ecumenism; and when it manages to get around to turning its face outwards to the world, it meddles in politics. Bishops who should be talking about God talk instead about the inner city. They neglect what ought to be their expertise to make fools of themselves in areas where they can only be amateurs.

Social concern – sign of a loss of nerve?

Christians who believe that it is perfectly possible to talk about God *and* the inner city, indeed that one cannot talk about the God and Father of our Lord Jesus Christ, without talking about the inner city, and can support this claim by taking a handful of episcopal sermons and showing that, while one percent may be about social concerns, ninety-nine percent are about sin, redemption and prayer, must at least pause and examine what justice there may be in this reaction against the "social gospel". It was not so many years ago that the Secular City was celebrated as the New Jerusalem, that, from a very superficial reading of Dietrich Bonhoeffer, some theological students gave up saying their prayers in the name of "religionless Christianity", that young clergymen strove to be social workers, and that it was thought better to speak of a "sick" society rather than a sinful one.

Without any doubt there has been a loss of nerve, a shrinking from the hard task of speaking of the great themes of faith in a way which engaged both the minds and imaginations of our contemporaries. It did not go without notice that if the preacher said something controversial about politics and spiced it with a denial of a few doctrines of the faith, then the media would bend to him their unstinted attention, while if he said that God was for real and the dying and rising of the Lord Jesus brought life in a way no political programme could, then his words would pass without comment. Indeed those who speak most loudly about the erosion of faith are, in part, victims of an illusion created by the media. While occasional outbursts of religious eccentricity have had more than enough attention, the still small voice of balanced faith has been neglected, thus giving a distorted picture of what is going on in Christianity. The sober truth is that, while the regular churchgoer will have heard many dull and dire sermons, he could count on the fingers of one hand the few which by any stretch of the imagination could be called controversial.

Committed to humanity because committed to God

However, let us be clear. We have no interest in a faith which is politically committed and religiously anaemic, no interest in one where "God talk" has become simply the decoration of a pale pink secular creed. The faith which we believe has a right to speak to our society is the catholic faith, that is the balanced whole faith, which is committed to the human task because it is committed to the mystery of God. It is this rich and integrated vision of the meaning of life which is able to fit together prayer and politics.

However in face of scepticism from without and scepticism from within, Christianity clearly cannot expect an automatic hearing when it claims to set goals for society. Inhabiting a pluralist society which has no one official set of values and is content to hold the ring for a number of competing claimants, our faith has to win its way. I suggest that, instead of starting with claims to divine authority which are precisely the claims which are questioned, instead of hurling at the world, the texts of Scripture or the teaching of the Church, we need to show that the enterprise of faith actually engages, and has always engaged, in the very conflicts to which our first chapter referred. Christianity, as a matter of fact, is not a stranger to the tensions between the individual liberty to flourish and the claims of the common life.

The common life of religion

Although it has been said that religion is what a man does with his loneness, religion is more obviously a social activity.

The raw materials on which any student of religion must work are those of common rituals and shared beliefs. If personal piety must be taken account of, it is always a personal piety which has been fostered by religion as a community activity. Because it is a community activity, religion acquires forms of organization and has an inescapably institutional aspect. Some form of regulation of the rituals evolves, some ordering of each holy occasion. A priesthood or an order of holy leaders soon emerges. Indeed it is very difficult to stop this happening. Religious groups such as the Quakers or House Churches which most cherish their "lay", unofficial, democratic and anti-institutional insights have a considerable struggle to maintain these consistently. The Society of Friends is not without its Meeting Houses and its forms of albeit unobtrusive leadership. The House Churches have thrown up some very authoritarian leaders and in some places have grown to the point where they have to hire cinemas on a Sunday morning to meet for worship.

The social ordering of faith

Of course the "social nature" of religion is to be seen most clearly in the so-called "main-stream" Churches. These are characterized by ordered ministries, forms of government and leadership. They are rooted in this world through their property and economic resources. Indeed these make up the obvious and visible faces of religion. Despite the protests of believers that there are things in the household of faith which go deeper and are more essential that the activities of councils and synods, popes and bishops, it is this visible tip of the iceberg which is in the public eye and which, for better or worse, provides the staple diet of media comment. Whatever else religion may be, it is clearly stuck into the mud of this life and therefore shares in some of the restrictions and possibilities of other social organizations.

In one way the particular social ordering of a religion helps to set it apart as something unique. It is a badge of identity.

Thus accepting the leadership of the Pope is as much a defining characteristic of the Roman Catholic Church as having special beliefs about Mary the Mother of Jesus. Thus the role of elders in the Presbyterian Church sets that Church apart as much as does its beliefs about predestination. But in another way these social orderings reveal the "earthiness" of Churches. The fact of being ordered, of being institutional relates them to other orders and other institutions. Far from floating above the social order, religion is affected by and affects it. Anyone reading the history of the Christian Church has to be prepared to encounter this overlap with the kingdom of this world; for this story is not simply the history of saints, it is also the very ambiguous history of the interaction between the community of faith and the society around it. We shall discover popes who have armies and are embroiled in the politics of Europe. We shall discover bishops who end up as senior civil servants. And we shall discover the other side of the coin, kings not so much interfering as quite naturally thinking it part of their responsibility to order the affairs of the Church. The truth is that the attempt to maintain a distinction between the secular and the sacred, between religion and politics is a comparatively new attempt, one born in part, of a weariness with the destructive and divisive influence of religion in politics.

The intermingling of sacred and secular

Thus what we see as a highly problematic matter was, to our forefathers, quite simple. For them religion and politics were inseparably intertwined. This did not mean that they were incapable of making any distinction between Church and state. They were. So kings probed away at the "benefit of clergy" which would seem to set "criminous clerks" above the law of the land. So popes resisted the claim of kings to appoint bishops to the highest ecclesiastical posts. Yet whatever borderline disputes there might be between king

41

and pope, between sacred and secular, it was generally recognized that all this took place within the context of Christendom. "Secular" did not have the connotation of unbelief. Sacred and secular were believed to be under the same God and concerned with the same "real" world.

Some will be quick to say that herein lie the seeds of the corruption of pure religion. Constantine's embracing of Christianity and its consequent elevation to become the "official" faith of the empire was an unqualified disaster both for society and the purity of religion. Instead of personal conviction and fervour came a tired and sometimes reluctant conformism. About the darker side of the "establishment" of Christianity there can be no denial and yet it was all surely much more ambiguous than that. If faith took the risk of getting its hands dirty then it was not without benefits to society. Unwanted children ceased to be abandoned and left to die, there was some softening in the treatment of prisoners, some advance in the care of the sick. Although there were proud prelates who delighted to be princes, there were others like Gregory the Great who more reluctantly shouldered the burdens of government in a decaying empire. Faltering, inadequate, fraught with peril though these attempts at involvement in human affairs might be, can we not catch in them some glimpse of that divine taking of responsibility for the world which is revealed in the incarnation? In all justice, it must be said that those Christian groupings who have striven most energetically to keep themselves free from being enmeshed in the world, have not always been most marked by Christ-like charity.

An intermingling central to the faith of the old covenant

Indeed this enmeshment in human affairs, the blurring of the boundaries between religion and politics is a central feature of Christianity's background. The faith of Jesus of Nazareth is a faith which has not cut away its Jewish roots but deliberately and lovingly treasured them. Its prayer-book is essentially the prayer-book of Judaism, the rich inheritance of the Psalms. The Old Testament it reads, not as a sort of introduction to the real business of Christianity, but as part of that Holy Scripture through which, it believes, the living God continues to address his people. There was an early heresy, that of Marcion, which pretended that Christians had got beyond the world of the Old Testament, indeed that the God and Father of the Lord Jesus Christ and the God of Abraham, Isaac and Moses were different gods. Probe the piety of those who turn their backs on "social" religion, and you will encounter echoes of this rejection of the Old Covenant.

The faith of Israel is wholehearted in its commitment to human affairs. Indeed it is a frequent cause of scandal to the spiritual that the Old Testament is so full of wars, revolutionary coups, political assassination, stories of social injustice and exhortations to more energetic wealth creation and to a fairer distribution of that wealth. The Old Testament is a very earthy, human set of books. Here is life as it really is, warts and all. But it is not without great flights of spirituality. Prayer and politics mingle precisely because it is believed that to understand the real world aright we have to wake up to the judgement and mercy of the unseen God in its midst.

An intermingling central to the faith of the new covenant

Is this holy secularism modified in the New Testament? Certainly the Kingdom which Jesus proclaims is not a political kingdom built up by the labour of human beings. It is God's rule to be perceived only by those who have eyes to see, a rule in this life often hidden and obscure, a rule whose earthly form is to be seen on Calvary, the place of shame and execution, the place where significantly the rulers of Church and state gang up to deny that reign. Christ's Kingdom is not our achievement, and yet it is not up in the skies out of reach. It is the Kingdom which descends to us, which comes down out of heaven as God's gift. The parables of the Lord are full of precisely that everyday earthy world which we have seen in the Old Testament. His almighty deeds through which the power of the Kingdom is shown are deeds which make fleshly existence anew. The New Creation may not have arrived in its fullness yet its birth pangs have begun. Even now we may taste the first-fruits of the harvest to come.

The community of those who have recognized the lordship of Jesus is believed to be a foretaste of the Kingdom. Of the baptized, St. Paul can say "if anyone is in Christ, there is a piece of new creation". Incredibly rich and bold images are used of this community, images like the Body and Vine which are essentially to do with the closeness of the relationship between believers and the mystery of God through Jesus of Nazareth. These are images which go to the centre of faith, the adoption of us men and women into the very love of God himself, so that we can be said to be partakers of the divine nature. And yet this flight of spirituality takes place without any loss of earthiness. For all this is about precisely the taking up of what is ordinary and worldly into that divine love. Thus the community of faith, as well as being the "mystical body" is also a human organization which can be studied by the sociologist. According to the Acts of the Apostles, we find the community struggling with problems familiar to any organization: qualifications for membership, the handling of its resources, its structure of decision-making and authority.

Liberty and community – tensions within the Church

Indeed the New Testament shows that as the community expands and becomes more than a sect within Judaism, it has an ever-growing problem of maintaining its shape and identity, of holding the show together. Inevitably there are disagreements about the message, about what the community stands for, and equally inevitably there is a tendency for these disagreements to harden into the setting up of rival bodies, each one of which, of course believes itself alone to be in possession of the "true faith". Sometimes the splits, the schisms, are because explorers of faith cut their roots with the flesh and blood past, whether of Judaism or Jesus of Nazareth, and advance to a "new" spirituality Sometimes they come about through "traditionalists" being locked into a conservation of the past, a refusal to take on board new questions and insights which engagement with Graeco-Roman culture necessitates.

The fundamental instinct of the community is that the brothers and sisters of the Lord Jesus should stay together through thick and thin. The bond of Christian love is held to be more important that the brightest of insights. Those who go out from amongst us, St. John says, go out because they never really belonged to us; that is, they never really grasped what this enterprise of love was about. But if it is love which holds the community together, that love has to be articulated in an institutional way. The spirit has to be made flesh in organization. Thus the later books of the New Testament already begin to show the development of bones and framework which will express this binding force. Settled expressions of faith and an order of leadership begin to emerge, not as a lapse into worldliness but as embodied bands of love.

As we said before, these bones which hold the show together mark out the Christian community with a particular shape and identity. They are the expression of a new organization. It was as such that Christianity came up against the Roman empire. While that empire was tolerant of personal faith and was able to absorb all manner of beliefs, it was very sensitive to organizations which seemed to constitute a threat to the state. The Governor Pliny thus writes anxiously to the Emperor Trajan about a private-enterprise initiative to set up a new fire brigade. Might this association with its internal rules and regulations be construed as a potential political menace? Now here were these Christians, who not only believed strange things, but who seemed to be of a "Third race" with a dangerously subversive organized common life. With its obstinate refusal to go through the formalities of the state religion and offer incense to Lord Caesar it was an even clearer political threat.

The responsibility of holiness

Yet this obstinate oddness – this consciousness of being a people set apart went along with that strong sense of social responsibility, that care for the ordering of this world which was part of its inheritance from Judaism. Even in the times of fiercest persecution, Christians were reminded to pray for the Emperor. They were to be marked out in the world as good citizens. The accusation of social irresponsibility is fiercely denied by Christian apologists.

"We are no Brahmins or Indian gymnosophists, who live in woods, and as it were in exile from other men", protests Tertullian, "we act as men under the warmest sense of gratitude to God our Lord, the Creator of all things; and we reject nothing he has made for the use of man."[1]

In the epistle to Diognetus it is argued that the very non-conformity, the distinctiveness of Christians, far from being world-denying is for the sake of the world:

. . .while living in Greek and barbarian cities and following the local customs . . .they show forth the wonderful and confessedly strange character of the constitution of their own citizenship. They dwell in their own fatherlands, but as if sojourners in them; they share all things as citizens, and suffer all things as strangers. Every foreign country is their fatherland, and every fatherland is a foreign country. . . .To put it shortly, what the soul is in the body, that the Christians are in the world.[2]

My concern has here been to show some grounds for paying

attention to what Christians might have to say about the problems of our society. Those grounds I hold to be that here is a body which, whatever else it might be, is an institution which embraces peoples of different nations and cultures and which has had a long history of wrestling with the problems of society, both in its own internal ordering and in its consistent concern for those societies in which it finds itself. The claim for attention is not on the basis of a particularly good and successful track record. We may learn as much from its failures as from its successes. The claim on our attention is simply on the basis of a long experience and on an evident zeal to reflect on that experience.

Freedom and the common good

We identified in our first chapter the perennial tussle between the claims of individual freedom to develop particular giftedness and the claims of the common good. The Christian Church is worth our attention for its painful experience of this.

Gifted individual against the community

One has only to consider those ecclesiastical issues which hit headlines to see how often this tussle is at their heart. Whether it is Rome in conflict with Archbishop Levebvre, or with a theologian like Hans Küng, the problem is essentially the same. Whether the rebel sails under "conservative" or "radical" colours, he possesses a burning conviction, a personal insight which comes into conflict with the official line. He believes that he is right and the position of the main body is either plain wrong or inadequate. Sometimes, as in the case of Archbishop Levebvre, this leads to expulsion of the dissident and the setting up a new body, which is always, of course, claimed by the dissident to be the one true and faithful body. At other times, indeed more frequently, some less drastic disciplining takes place and a *modus vivendi* of varying degrees of discomfort is allowed.

Indeed both parties to the conflict have an interest in staying together. Dissidents are often amongst the most enthusiastic members of the community. They would not wrestle so hard and go through the bothersome business of conflict did they not have a deep care for it. The community in turn recognizes the giftedness of its rebel sons and daughters. If it is alert to its own history, it will know that very often the rebels of one age become the pillars of orthodoxy of the next. It needs this giftedness and, when it is strong and secure, works hard to retain the rebel within the fold. Conversely heresy-hunts and expulsions are signs of community weakness and fear.

Small community against large community

Sometimes the conflict is less between the freedom of the gifted individual and the community, than between the smaller community and the bigger one. The freedom to flourish is here claimed by a sub-grouping which believes itself to be in possession of a corporate insight. This, in turn may generate further dissent within the smaller grouping so that there may be rebels against the rebels who may align themselves with the views of the wider community. Something of this is involved in the Anglican Communion's agonies over the ordination of women to the priesthood and the episcopate. Some smaller communities, provinces and national groupings of that communion, have claimed the right to pursue their conviction that such ordinations should take place. But, because this conviction is not shared by all provinces, there is tension and a straining of the bonds which hold the Anglican Communion together. Indeed, for Anglicanism with its historic roots in the Reformation assertion of local autonomy over against the central power of the Papacy, the peculiar problem is the structuring of this wider, universal community in such a way as to justify speaking of the particular identity of the thing called "Anglicanism".

Christian unity – the loss of variety?

Such conflicts between the lesser community and the greater are writ large in the struggle for Christian unity. Is such a thing possible except by way of a take-over by the larger partner? Can the claims of a wider community be reconciled with the preservation of the particular giftedness of those communities at present separated? It is to be noted that the smaller the community is, the more sensitive it is to such problems. The large partner opens its arms and is peculiarly insensitive to the fact that its loving embrace could spell the death of the particular identity which has held the loyalty of the members of this smaller group. Such identities are made up, not simply of special beliefs, but also of patterns of worship and quite subtle matters of style of life and ways of doing, what on the surface, seem quite unimportant things. Churches are complex packages of belief and action, possessing a particular flavour. All this is part of what is accounted the "giftedness" of each Church. The fear is that the big partner will simply absorb the smaller, with the result that all such richness and variety will be lost. The "great Church" will be a dull, grey, monochrome organization, something less interesting and vital than the separate parts which have gone to make it up. The central task of the search for a valid unity is thus the search for a belonging together which will preserve and enhance the variety which has been valued in separation.

Variety against unity – a perennial problem

Handling rebels, reconciling the local to the universal Church, embracing lively variety within wider unity – such issues make up newspaper headlines on contemporary ecclesiastical affairs. The slightest acquaintance with Church history will show that these themes are perennial. Whether it is the sixteenth-century affirmation of the independence of the local Church, the assertion of national Christian identity against what seemed to be the reforming inertia of a centralized Papacy, or whether it is the later more radical cry for individual religious liberty, the liberty of private judgement and the right to worship as one pleases, the tensions are basically the same as those which confront Christians today. Will the particular flavour and style of religious sub-groupings be allowed to flourish or will they get squashed out by centralism? Will the particular giftedness of the awkward squad become an occasion of division and the setting up of a rival show, or can the universal Church have the wit, foresight and skill to retain this giftedness for its own enrichment? Will the freedom to flourish lead men like Wycliffe and Huss into the wilderness, to suffering and death or will it lead others like Thomas Aquinas and Francis of Assisi into becoming the honoured enrichers of the main stream? The gulf between heretic and Church hero is a narrow one. What makes it possible for the common life to lose one and retain the other?

Variety against unity – a New Testament problem

Such perennial themes, the conflict between the individual liberty to flourish and the common life of the body, reach right back into the pages of the New Testament. Gone are the days when we were able to read the story of the early Church as one of all sweetness and light. The Church emerges with a strong common life as articulated in Luke's description of the result of Pentecost:

> . . .all who believed were together and had all things in common; and they sold their possessions and goods and distributed them to all, as any had need. And day by day attending the temple together and breaking bread in their homes, they partook of food with glad and generous hearts, praising God and having favour with all the people (Acts 2:44–47).

However idealized, Luke's picture bears witness to the reality

50

of an identifiable community. And yet what a variety of giftedness this community throws up! The very gospels themselves resist the portrait of Jesus being reduced to a dull monochrome photograph. Each gospel presents a particular picture, is written from a unique standpoint. The rest of the New Testament literature is equally rich in variety – presenting not simply the genius of gifted individuals like Paul and John, but whole communities touched by their genius and possessing different styles of life and leadership. The inevitable conflicts are not evaded. The Corinthian church seems to have been a hotbed of party strife. The Apostle Paul had a stand-up fight with the leader of the Apostles, Peter (Galatians 2:11). The tensions with which the Church lives today and has lived throughout its history have been there from the beginning.

Resolving the problem – the Pauline solution

In his first letter to the Corinthians St. Paul faces up to these realities and proposes at least the terms in which there is to be resolution of conflict. It has been reported to him, that there are dissensions in Corinth – not any old quarrelling, but high minded stuff, "I belong to Paul", "I belong to Apollos", "I belong to Cephas". This, says the Apostle, should not be. "You are to be united in the same mind and the same judgement" (1 Corinthians 1:10ff.). The whole letter circles around the community problem of allowing the gifted to flourish while retaining this flourishing for the common good. The strong minded, who know perfectly well that food dedicated to idols is, in Christian terms, just food, have to have a care for the "weaker brethren" who are still haunted by the old superstitions.

No, this does not mean a taming of genius, strength and initiative, a levelling down to the grey mediocrity of an allegedly "simple faithful". "There are varieties of gifts". "The body does not consist of one member but many". Indeed the whole burden of chapter 12 is the argument that though

51

there is but one body, this does *not* mean a lack of variety. The united community requires a variety of giftedness. It cannot work without this.

If the whole body were an eye, where would be the hearing? If the whole body were an ear, where would be the sense of smell? But, as it is, God arranged the organs in the body, each one of them, as he chose. If all were a single organ, where would the body be? As it is, there are many parts, yet one body (1 Corinthians 12:14ff).

The reconciliation of this freedom to flourish and the claims of community, comes through the pursuit of the "still more excellent way", the way of love (1 Corinthians 13). It is when the gifted use their gifts for the service of others, that freedom and community are reconciled.

Clearly this Pauline recipe for reconciliation needs to be explored in further depth and related to the over-all pattern of Christian living and belief. We shall have more to say on this in the next two chapters. Here we are content to rest our case, not by parading alleged solutions to social problems, but with the simple claim that this Christian thing has a word to speak because for nearly two thousand years it has endured such problems, been scarred by them and yet reflected on them. It may not speak from success, but at least it speaks from experience – in fact considerably longer experience than that of any existing political party.

Notes

1. Tertullian, *Apology* 42.
2. *Epistle to Diognetus* 5,6.

THREE

THE PATH TO HUMAN FULFILMENT – FROM DEPENDENCE TO INDEPENDENCE

The Christian claim to be able to contribute to the debate on freedom and the community will be made, not on the grounds of an appeal to the authority of God, but on the grounds that here is a community which has had some experience of living with this conflict and being forced to reflect on it. Such a modest claim does not mean that we renounce the cry "Thus said the Lord" but that we recognize that we shall not be able to enter into dialogue with our contemporaries, for whom "the word of the Lord" is of doubtful meaning, simply by an appeal to "outside" authority. The only way in which we can hope that this authority can make sense is by presenting our community's vision of freedom and community and showing that its coherence ultimately depends on its rootedness in the reality of the mystery of God.

The search for mature independence

As we said, the facts of life are the facts of interdependence. No life stands on its own feet. Everywhere we look we see complicated patterns of interdependence and we begin to discover, through bitter experience, that the destruction of such patterns has widespread disrupting results. The destruction of rain forests in South America can bring climatic changes throughout the world. Even my deodorant or my fly spray can, it seems, punch a hole in the ozone layer. Such interdependence is a fact of human life. We are born totally dependent on the care of other human beings. The infant can scrabble up no ladder by itself. Our human story is one of a long and painful struggle for independence followed by an equally long struggle to accept the joys and responsibilities of interdependence.

It is important to be clear that the dependency with which we start and for which we aim are not the same. We struggle out of our immature dependence to be free to be ourselves and not just an extension of our parents. There is to be no going back on this, no retreat into the womb of a dependency existence. Yet our maturity is not reached at the stage of immature independence, of adolescent rebellion against parental authority, or where the young adult has broken free to stand on his own feet. Beyond this beckons the goal of entering – now freely and as a unique individual, capable of giving the self which has been wrested from the bonds of dependency – into relationships with other, into patterns of interdependent living. The goal is to love and be loved; that is, to enjoy the giving and receiving of interdependence.

This distinction between immature and mature dependence is essential to our understanding of the problem of our society. A "dependency culture" could be a very immature culture, the result perhaps of a bewildering and complicated world in which people are tempted to sink back into the arms of a benevolent maternal state. It could, on the other hand, be a very mature culture whose adherents had got beyond the adolescent conflict between desire to boost the ego and the fearful flight back to security and had reached the stage when the joys of giving and receiving in community seemed more substantial than the pursuit of a jealously guarded private path. It might just be that people saw that "private affluence and public squalor" were not quite good enough, that the rich society was shamed by the presence of the homeless living in cardboard boxes or by the decay of public services, so that a pound extra in the health service or in education might be worth more than a pound in the pocket. The first is a retreat, the second an advance. We shall distinguish the two by calling the first a "dependency culture" and the second an "interdependency culture".

The biblical priority of human solidarity

Something of this going forward, this pilgrimage into interdependence, is articulated in the Christian message and way. The starting point for faith is the fact of dependence. Throughout the Bible the story of faith is a story about a "people", about human solidarity. Thus the Old Testament concerns the dealings of God with his chosen people the Jews and the New Testament concerns what is claimed to be the New Israel, the Christian Church. Those self-same scriptural writings are more than the products of isolated individual geniuses; they reflect the life of communities in which, of course, gifted individuals played an important part. Before the scriptures there was the community. These writings did not remain frozen in hallowed finality. They were put to use by the community, worked on, knocked about, edited and re-edited by different generations.

This priority of human solidarity, the fact of men and women being bound up in the bundle of life with each other, is fundamental to an understanding of Christian faith. Of course sometimes this is expressed in ways which seem offensive to our ears. Who wants to believe in the jealous God who visits "the iniquities of the fathers upon the children to the third and fourth generations"? Who can fail to be horrified at the fate of Korah whose rebellion against Moses is punished by the destruction, not only of the offender himself, but with him the wives and families of all his associates (Numbers 16)? Yet, stripped of all crude notions

55

of divine retribution, this sense of human interconnectedness makes good although hard sense for us who know only too clearly that the bitter harvest of individual offences is often reaped by the innocent. What of the victims of the AIDS virus, what of those caught up in the dreadful chain of child-abuse? Who is punished more, the convicted prisoner or his wife and family? The Bible's sense of human solidarity is true to our experience of life. We are not self-made; for good or ill we effect one another.

Solidarity in evil

It is the sense of no man being an island which is carried into Christian faith in its doctrines of sin and redemption. We cannot explain our experience of evil in this world simply in terms of individual wrong choices. Personal responsibility is, as we shall see, an essential part, but it is not the whole story for we are not launched into life with a clean slate. Each individual starts with a particular genetical inheritance and is thrust into a particular environment. Indeed all of us, without asking, are placed in a world which is in a state of rebellion against its Creator, a world which is bent and twisted by that rebellion. Thus, says St. Paul in Romans 7, it is not merely a matter of deciding to be good and then forthwith doing it. The fact is: "I do not understand my own actions. For I do not do what I want, but I do the very thing that I hate." I am dragged down by the sin which "dwells within me", by some alien force which my ideals reject.

All this is a shrewd analysis of what is common experience and what is shown in dramatic form in the book of Genesis. Adam chooses to do the forbidden thing but before he chooses he is enticed, not only by Eve, but by the Serpent in the garden. Evil goes before us. Evil is in the atmosphere we breathe from the day of our birth. Sentiment may be offended by the bleak assertion that the new-born child is "born in sin" and it would rightly be offended if this were taken to mean that the child had consciously chosen evil, but, as a sober statement of the reality of being thrust into a bent world, it is plain truth.

I am talking about Original Sin, the one doctrine that trendy pale pink clerics are alleged not to believe in. It is one of the curiosities of our present situation that it is those who believe most firmly in individual responsibility who are most insistent on reminding dreamy idealists that we all live in a "fallen world", that is a world afflicted by such "original sin". In truth no doctrine so firmly cuts at the roots of unbridled individualism, no doctrine so disturbs the naive cry of Rousseau that "man is born free". If, as those of the political Right are for ever saying, we should be hearing more about "sin", then they will have to brace themselves to hear the austere voice of orthodoxy which says: "Man is born in chains and everywhere awaits the glorious liberty of the children of God."

Solidarity the starting point and goal

However this reality of being thrust into solidarity by the facts of my birth is for good and well as ill. The Bible's first words about solidarity are about the Creator's recognition that "it is not good that a man should be alone" (Genesis 2:18) and thus, in the gift of Eve, a recognition of the deepest level of human interdependence. The intention of God in creation is that people should live in harmony, not only amongst themselves but also with the created order and above all with their Creator. God looks out over this world of interdependence and says "Behold it is very good", and that goodness remains the fundamental truth. Sin has disfigured the image of God in humanity but it has not destroyed it. If we are thrust into a sin-orientated environment, we are to know that the "real world" cannot be dismissed as "nasty and brutish" and accordingly fitted out with political systems suited to such existence. This world, scarred by sin, remains a theatre of divine grace. God is as work in it and his work of restoration or redemption is not a plucking of individuals from a sin-stained environment into some privatized heaven where he and the soul can be locked in private discourse, but the gift of the New City, the new solidarity of Jerusalem. For the end of humanity as for the beginning, it is not good for us to be alone. Moreover the means to this end, the instrument of this salvation, is also a solidarity, the new solidarity of the People of God reborn in Jesus. But more of this later. Here it is enough to insist that the Bible's insistence on human solidarity which initially strikes us as crude and barbaric remains an integral part of the Christian vision and way. Development of course there is, but it is not a development from crude corporatism into pure individualism.

The reality of individual responsibility and freedom

However the question of individual responsibility and freedom has to be faced. Are we, at the end of the day, just puppets on a string, carried by one environment or another? Have we any genuine choice or are we simply pushed around, whether by enticing evil or divine grace? Here we have to say that the Bible sees a genuine development of understanding of individual worth and value. There is a movement out of immature dependency, through independence to mature interdependence. This is most clearly shown in St. Paul's letter to the Galatians, a fiery manifesto, in which the coming of Christ is announced as the moment of radical freedom. We were once minors, under the care of a tutor, as far as rights are concerned no better than slaves, but now we have become sons and heirs. "For freedom Christ has set us free; stand fast therefore, and do not submit again to the yoke of slavery" (Galatians 5:1).

But of course we do not have to wait for St. Paul to discover the biblical emphasis on the responsibility and dignity of the individual human person. There is a classical statement in Ezekiel 18. "The fathers have eaten sour grapes, and the children's teeth are set on edge" (verse 1). Such was the current saying pointing up the reality of human interdependence. Yet, the prophet complains, it is misused to dodge individual responsibility. And he encounters this danger with the assertion: "The soul that sins shall die. The son shall not suffer for the iniquity of the father, nor the father suffer for the iniquity of the son." Indeed "if a wicked man turns away from all his sins . . . and keeps my statutes and does what is lawful and right, he shall surely live; he shall not die" (verses 20–21).

This sense of personal responsibility is reflected in the whole ethical tradition of the Old and New Testaments. Life presents us with choices. I am constantly standing at the crossroads at which I must decide whether to follow the way of God which leads to life or the way of evil which leads to death. At such crossroads I am not able to invoke my genetic inheritance or the influence of my environment. I stand in this sense alone, having to choose for myself. No doubt we are not often conscious of the solemnity of such choices, so that the Day of Judgement, the moment of truth, will find us saying that we never realized the issues were as serious as this. In Matthew 25 both the righteous and the unrighteous are surprised to learn that in serving or failing to serve the needy they have been dealing with Christ himself. Yet whether conscious or not the choice has been made, a choice of eternal significance, which leads to the fateful separation of sheep and goats. The terrifying truth about the parable of the rich man who allowed the beggar Lazarus to lie neglected at his gates is that "the great gulf" which is discovered between the former tormented in Hades and the latter living it up in Abraham's "bosom", is a gulf which the rich man has dug by his indifference in this life. Those who acquiesce in social division, who fail to recognize another human being as brother, fashion division for all eternity.

The reality of personal responsibility emphasises individual dignity. The Christian doctrines of heaven and hell sharpen this. What I do here and now does not simply effect the shape of my life and that of others at this moment, it has consequences for my final end, for my ultimate fulfilment. I can throw it all away, choose to be wrapped up in deadly self-regard. All this, which is Hell, comes, not because I am thrust down into disaster by an avenging God offended that I have broken his rules, but because I have chosen thus to turn my back on love and have gone on so choosing. Such is my ability to choose, such is my dignity, that no paternalist welfare God will snatch away my freedom and insist on imposing his Heaven because "I don't really know what is good for me."

In the Catholic Church this taking of personal responsibility is embodied in the sacrament of reconciliation. The penitent comes to the sacrament to receive, not the forgiveness of the priest, but of God whose instrument the priest is. But first the penitent confesses before the priest his or her sins. There is a particularity about this, the nailing of a vague feeling of being wrong with God, to certain things done, said and thought which are wrong and, perhaps far more significantly, good things left undone. In this recognition that I am to blame − through my fault, my own fault, my own most grievous fault − I discover my dignity as a person, know myself to be free and responsible.

The value of the individual person

It is in the context of such a sharp emphasis on personal responsibility that Jesus teaches how the individual matters to God. While we are not to fear those who can kill the body, we are to fear him "who has the power to cast into hell" (Luke 12:4−5). But this "holy fear" is not just the result of the threat of punishment, it springs from the recognition of how much we, and what we do, matter to God. "Are not five sparrows sold for two pennies? And not one of them is forgotten before God. Why, even the hairs of your head are all numbered. Fear not; you are of more value than many sparrows"(Luke 12:6−7).

What Jesus teaches that he also practises. We find him in the gospels surrounded by crowds, yet he is constantly spotting the face in the crowd, plucking out now this individual, now that, to bend on this one person his entire concentration. Little Zaccheus lost in the crowd, having to climb a tree to be seen, the blind beggar Bartimaeus, elbowed aside, told to be silent, both are spotted by the Lord and attended to (Mark 9:45ff.).

If it is a mark of personal worth and dignity to exercise responsibility in freedom, that worth and dignity do not depend on such an exercise. We are not valued by God because we choose wisely and do well, rather we are enabled to choose wisely and do well because we are valued by God. This is absolutely fundamental to the gospel and thus to an understanding of Christian humanism. The Lord does not concentrate on the virtuous to award them his gifts. He is typically to be found amongst taxgatherers and sinners. The lavishing of God's gifts come first and the call to the holiness of grateful living comes afterwards. Everything rests on the divine giving, or grace.

This is very difficult for us to grasp, for we insist on God acting within the rather restricted limits of our understanding of "fairness". People, we think, are valuable for what they do with their lives. They become valuable because they are clever, or hard-working, or good. You have only to hear the worried reaction of a congregation to the parable of the labourers in the vineyard (Matthew 20:1–16). The idea that those who had worked only one hour should be paid the same as those who had borne the burden and heat of the whole day continues to offend. "It is not fair", the cry goes up. Of course that is precisely the point. God smashes through the wages barrier, goes beyond fairness and lavishes his largesse on all. We are recipients of his love simply because we are his valued children. Our worth is established not by what we do but by what God has made us be. The parable thus ends with God asking us: "Do you begrudge my generosity?"

Individual value – the foundation of true equality

This is the foundation of the Christian understanding of human equality. It has nothing at all to do with the absurd pretence that everyone is the same – equally clever, equally hard working, equally good. All the rich variety of human giftedness is accepted. A belief in equality springs from seeing with the eyes of God, a "seeing" which rejoices in this variety, and yet sees beyond to the one fundamental thing, that this person is an infinitely precious child of God. Compared with this mountainous fact all the inequalities of life are trivial molehills. It is the simple perception that, in the end, people are just people and that nothing matters more than that.

It is important to notice where I have located this understanding of equality. I have placed it, not in the context of solidarity, but in the context of individual worth and freedom. It is because it is too often placed in the former context that we get into all sorts of muddles and misunderstandings about what it is to believe in equality. By grounding it in the fact of human interdependence, by making it a community rather than individual value, we find ourselves in the dreary business of resenting variety and holding back individual giftedness and flourishing for the sake of the common life. Levelling down becomes the inevitable name of the game and the colour of life a uniform greyness. Freedom is seen to be in opposition to equality, and the art of social life a sort of balancing act, in which there is either too much freedom which will lead to "inequality" or too much equality which will inhibit freedom.

Now I am not pretending that such balancing acts do not have to be made. Acceptable forms of taxation are very much a matter of achieving such balance. However I think it is unhelpful to start with a bogus ideological conflict. It is perfectly possible to believe both in the equal value of each individual person and in the freedom of each individual person to flourish and become fulfilled. In fact the former, far from being in conflict with the latter, demands it. If I am truly affirming the value of each unique person, I shall also want that person to be free to be fully him or her self.

Certainly this is what Christians have seen to be the corollary of their understanding of the equality of the children of God. For St. Paul "sameness" is not to be characteristic of the community he dares to call the Body of Christ. "The body does not consist of one member, but of many". There are "a variety of gifts". "If all were a single organ where would the body be?" "As it is, God arranged the organs in the body, each one of them, as he chose" (1 Corinthians 12).

Witness of personal religion to the value of the individual

This perception of individual uniqueness goes deep. All members of the community are called to be saints, that is, to be reshaped to the form of Christ, for in him we see the new humanity. But this does not mean that saints pour off some conveyor belt mass-made and all looking the same. Each one is individually crafted, shaped and moulded by the living Holy Spirit, out of the particular material and circumstances of this life. Grace, it is said, perfects nature, by which we mean that God in his refashioning of us respects the givenness of unique lives.

People do not talk so much these days about "personal religion". That is a pity, because there is no way the individual can shuffle off his personal responsibility to respond to God onto the community. Each one of us has a unique vocation, a summons to follow along a particular path which will be trodden by no one else. This is why "personal prayer" can never be subsumed in that liturgical prayer where we join with others. That joining together, as we shall soon see, is of the greatest importance, but we have to be able to come to it not as liturgical robots but as those able to contribute the unique riches of a personal pilgrimage into God.

Faith's realism about freedom

So we return to our understanding of "freedom". St. Paul, as we said, is passionate about freedom and, in his letter to the Galatians, is fighting to prevent Christians from falling back into slavery, retreating from the maturity of sons and heirs into the immaturity of the child with his tutors and guardians. Certainly our faith treats us as responsible adults. We have sufficient freedom to choose what is right or what is wrong. Yet to leave it there would be superficial and unrealistic. If we measure freedom by our ability to manoeuvre, to decide from a wide range of options, we have to grant that some are more free than others. Certain physical disabilities remove or impair my ability to do certain physical tasks – perhaps to go rock climbing or to play a musical instrument. Brought up in the inner city, I shall be less free to become a lover of the countryside. Brought up in the depth of the country, I shall be less free to be a frequent theatre-goer. And then of course there is money – money which purchases an ever wider range of things and experiences to choose from.

People who exalt the virtue of freedom are often startlingly naive about its possession. They seem to think that we all start the race of life from the same point, with the same "amount" of freedom. Of course this is not the case. In the supermarket of life, some have more freedom to fill their shopping trolleys than others. So there is a certain realism about the Christian refusal to join hands and cry with Rousseau: "Man is born free". Instead the Christian sees freedom as the tantalising goal, that for which we seek, that for which we have to struggle. It is sensitive and alert to our unfreedom, to those points where we are tied, restricted and enslaved; and it is committed to the task of enlarging freedom, liberating people from whatever holds them back from flourishing and fulfilment.

The liberating work of God

Jesus, says St. Luke, when he came to his home-town of Nazareth, stood up in the synagogue and read from the prophet Isaiah:

> The Spirit of the Lord is upon me, because he has anointed me to preach good news to the poor.
> He has sent me to proclaim release to the captives and recovering of sight to the blind,
> to set at liberty those who are oppressed.
> "Today", said Jesus, "this scripture has been fulfilled in your hearing" (Luke 4:16ff.).

This calling to set free is not a mere matter of words. Jesus breaks into the securely guarded mansion of Satan to ransack his house and set his victims free. The sick are set free from disease, the poor are set free from hunger, the lonely and despised are liberated from social ostracism.

God does not overlook our material bondages yet, as he liberates from these, he makes such liberation point forward to the climax of liberation, the setting of us free from bondage to ourselves. God knows that it is good for us to be well-fed, well-housed, to be healthy and happy and yet he knows too that when we have enough and more than enough to eat, when the mortgage is paid off and we are in good company, we can still be unfulfilled and miserable as sin. For we can still be the prisoner of sin. Indeed, according to Jesus, our fundamental freedom is more threatened by wealth than by poverty. The affluent society is in greater danger of Hell than a Third World peasant society. "How hard it will be for those who have riches to enter the Kingdom of God" (Mark 10:23). Our Liberation Theology is incomplete if it does not realize that the heart of our human problem is this slavery to self, this failure to be open to our neighbour and open to the mystery of God. It is incomplete if it leaves us with a redeemer releasing us from the ills that flesh is heir to and does not press on to

Calvary where the Liberator fights his final battle, achieves his greatest work by going to the heart of our problem.

Freedom for what?

So for faith it is not enough to list what we need to be free *from*, we need above all the vision of what God calls us to be free *for*, a vision of what it is to be a fulfilled person. Here it is that those who bang the drum most vigorously for freedom are so pitifully inadequate. It is not the vigour of their libertarianism which we could challenge but the anaemic nature of what they take to be liberty. Freedom is reduced to the ability to choose from the widest possible range of goods. "The more you are able to have, the more freedom you possess" – such is the message. And the package is certainly dressed up in an alluring fashion.

> "Let no one dictate to you what you ought to choose. Reject all paternalist attempts to impose on you what is alleged to be good for you. Here on the shelves is the full range of goods which includes a delicious variety of beliefs and values. It is up to you to have what you wish."

And yet who stocks the shelves, who chooses what shall be on the shelves, who, in fact, is the new evangelist pouring money into his mission to tell you what it is that you need? It is not just religion which is telling us what we should do with our freedom but all sorts of vested interests parading styles of life as distinctive as that of the narrowest of religious sects. On inspection the "open cheque" understanding of freedom, that which says that freedom is simply the ability to choose whatever we want, is bogus. The real world is that of persuaders whose interests lie in edging us into quite definite patterns of living.

This is not to say that the simple ability to choose is not, in itself, a good thing. The life of the poor is a life which is largely determined from outside. Where you live, what job is available, what education you can have, what health services are to hand — all these are severely limited. Poverty can be measured in terms of such lack of opportunity to make choices which, of course, are far more significant for human happiness than the lack of ability to drink good wines and eat pheasant instead of mutton. Enlarging choice must, in itself, be a good thing. Yet, what I have called "fundamental freedom", does not necessarily follow from this. People can seem amazingly fulfilled and happy under the most restricting conditions. They have learned the art of "making the best of things" and that best is rather more than a lethargic despairing contentment. It is a discovery of "fundamental freedom" within the confines of restriction. Conversely, those who have the world at their feet, who can choose almost anything they want, can seem depressingly weighed down, submerged beneath abundance.

The freedom of Jesus

When I read the gospels I am struck both by the limitations laid on Jesus and yet by his extraordinary sense of freedom. He is brought up in a very parochial village at Nazareth. He is the carpenter's son. His extraordinary mission is packed into a brief three years or so. Even that mission has self-imposed limits. It is, in the first place, to "the lost sheep of the House of Israel". Any spilling over to the Gentiles is a bonus, an extra, a falling of crumbs from the table for the dogs to eat. If the time is short, the space is also confined. The man who is now in Capernaum cannot be, at the same time, in Jerusalem. There does not seem to be any planning, any proper attempt to maximise his "impact", to make sure that in such a brief time his message can get to the maximum number. The whole enterprise reaches its climax in the catastrophic unfreedom of captivity and execution. The condemned man hustled by the authorities to the gallows is the ultimate in loss of liberty.

And yet in all this there is an astonishing sense of "fundamental freedom". Jesus seems unpressured by lack of time, unconfined by the tiny area in which he must operate. He does not kick against the limitations or thrash around as a mere rebel. He has mastered the art of taking the restrictions and harnessing them to freedom. Thus he is not in rebellion against the faith and customs of the community in which he had been brought up. He accepts them all, indeed he loves them and by this makes all things new, fashioning them into instruments of liberty. The Sabbath is no longer to be defined in terms of restriction, what people are not allowed to do, but in terms of liberty, so that it is reborn as the day which points forward to the freedom of God's Kingdom. It is thus to be celebrated here and now by the setting free of Satan's victims. Finally, he does not rebel against the cup of suffering, and so the place of crucifixion becomes the place of ultimate freedom. Here, nailed to the wood, he freely gives himself to the Father and for his brothers and sisters. They might bind his hands and his feet, but they could not bind his love.

To be free for one another

All of which brings us to the centre of what the Christian understanding of freedom is about. It is freedom *for* love. Our salvation is precisely our being caught up in that unbound love of the Son of God. I said earlier on that St. Paul's letter to the Galatians can be called our "manifesto" of freedom. "For freedom Christ has set us free". Having been set free, the apostle says there is no going back. It is our duty to seize the dignity and responsibility God has given us. To use faith as a flight back to the womb, as a descent into immature irresponsibility is to have got it all wrong. "You were called to freedom, brethren". But the call is to "fundamental freedom", it is more than a heady shaking off of the shackles of restrictions, it is entry into the glorious liberty of the children of God. So there is the clear warning that libertarianism is not enough: "Do not use you freedom as an opportunity for the flesh, but through love be servants of one another. For the whole law is fulfilled in one word, 'You shall love your neighbour as yourself' " (Galatians 5:13–14). And so the Apostle makes his famous contrast between the way of the flesh and the way of the Spirit. The first with its "free" choice of immorality, impurity, licentiousness, jealousy, dissension and so on, is in fact the entry into a new slavery. The second, the way of the Spirit of Freedom, is characterized by love, joy, peace, patience, kindness and so on (Galatians 5:19–23). In other words the right sort of freedom is that which builds up community, the wrong sort that of selfish individualism. In Christian terms, freedom, far from living in tension or in contradiction with solidarity, exists for this, demands this. Our fulfilment, our maturity as human beings lies in the discovery and living out of our interdependence.

FOUR

THE PATH TO FULFILMENT – FROM INDEPENDENCE TO INTERDEPENDENCE

It is insufficient to define "freedom" in terms of "doing what I want to do". Certainly there has to be the basic freedom from restraint so that I can make a truly personal choice. But what I choose is not from an unlimited menu. Everyone grants this point. I may not choose to do what hurts my neighbour and so restricts his or her freedom. But am I then free to "hurt" myself? Consistent libertarians answer "Yes" to this and will thus oppose what they see as the "nanny" state from placing helmets on motor-bike riders, insisting on compulsory seat-belts in cars and restricting my freedom to harm myself through tobacco, drink and other drugs. Moreover they will ask the very pertinent question: "Where shall the state's zeal to preserve me from myself stop?" Who is to define what is "good" for me and what "bad" for me? Who has the right to make this definition? Formerly religious societies held that the greatest harm to the individual and to society was the erroneous thinking of heresy. Society, it was thought, had to be protected from deviant thinking and the individual had to be protected from himself. In more recent years we have seen this tradition of imposed healthy thought continued in marxist regimes.

Christianity goes to the centre of the problem by seeing

that the freedom to choose to do what I want to do can still be radical slavery – indeed the bitterest slavery of all. As long as I am simply choosing what I want I am in slavery to myself. The only way out of this ultimate imprisonment is through the movement forward into love, to the point where I seek not only my good but that of others. The goal of freedom is thus love. Emerging from dependence upon my parents, I painfully establish my own identity and become capable of free action. Make no mistake about it, this stage of independence is absolutely necessary. Without it there cannot be love, but only a slipping back into a dependency relationship in which true love cannot be found for I have not established the "self" to give in love.

The fear of going forward

This "slipping back" remains a real possibility both for us as individuals and as societies. The cry that "Man has come of age" is profoundly misleading. All the time we stand on that dangerous knife-edge where we can either step forward beyond independence or fall back into some comfortable womb. We are always in this danger because freedom is both infinitely desirable and terrifying. That "Yes", that "I will", that word of decision which will commit me for life can be evaded and I can either remain stuck at the stage of independence or I can return to undemanding immaturity, handing myself over to be carried by the system, the party, yes, the religion.

In much sexual promiscuity there is this fear of mature commitment, the fear of stepping forward out of my lone world to enter into a loving stable relationship with another. Can the other be really trusted? Can I trust myself? Better retain our separate identities than risk them being lost in the two becoming one flesh. I remain stuck in independence.

Or, of course, I can take a step back into immature dependence. It really is a very attractive option. I have seen mature men come to seminaries and within that ordered structured life revert to a childishness which to the outside observer seems astonishing. I have seen men held together and apparently flourishing within the order of service life, who simply come to pieces when faced with the necessity of standing on their own feet in civilian life. I have seen the inmates of prisons become unhealthily content within the austere disciplined yet secure life "inside". Prisons, it has been said, are the ultimate in the dependency culture.

It is very important then that we distinguish carefully between this immature dependency out of which we should grow yet back into which we can slide, and the dependency of maturity. It is clear beyond all doubt that religion can foster immature dependency, allowing grown adults, not only to sing, but to act out the hymn "we are but little children weak"! All that patronizing talk about "the simple faithful" who have to be shielded by their pastors from the slings and arrows of the devil, is but part of a dependency religion. "Mother Church" acts as the possessive mother, clutching children to her bosom, not letting them do the risky things like riding the bicycles of modern thought or hiking through the rough wild mountains of contemporary life. She will create a warm and homely ghetto from which she hopes her sons and daughters will not be tempted to rove.

A model for the letting-go of love

Mother Church, in Catholic thought, centres around Mary, the Mother of our Lord. Her love for her Son was warm and supportive, it created the environment of security in which as man he learned to walk freely in this world. But this love was not possessive. At great cost to herself, involving the piercing of her heart, Mary allowed her Son to "be about his Father's business", to go out from her into loneliness, danger, suffering and death (Luke 2:35, 41–52). There is a particularly tough maternal love which lets the son be to pursue such a path of peril, never to call him back. It means terrible suffering, a suffering made worse because the lover must always keep her distance and not intrude. Mary cannot be on the Cross but only at the foot of it. Here is the model for Mother Church, the model which spells death to the fostering of immature dependency by fussy anxious ecclesiastics.

But instead of losing freedom by the retreat back into immature dependence or remaining stuck in sterile independence, the individual can advance to mature interdependence, tasting the freedom to love. I can be built into that Human Arch through which my weakness thrown onto the weakness of another is converted into strength. Yes, love requires both giving and receiving, outgoing generosity but also the willingness to be the recipient. Such is the advance beyond independence to interdependence.

The way of faith as the way of solidarity

Some religions have seen the destiny of humanity as purely individual pilgrimage – "the flight of the lone to the alone". Of such religion it can be said that it is a matter "between myself and my Maker". In contrast the Christian faith insists that the way of salvation is the way of "communion", belonging or solidarity. That is: I cannot find my personal fulfilment as a free and responsible person save by advancing beyond independence to mature dependence on God and beyond isolation into the give and take of the Christian community.

The model for such mature interdependence is given in Jesus of Nazareth who is the Second Adam, the prototype of humanity. As I said in the last chapter, even the most casual reader of the gospels comes away with the impression of his extraordinary freedom. Although rooted in the faith and customs of his people, he is never imprisoned by convention. Those customs through which timid religion seeks to protect "the godly" from contamination by "the ungodly" are thrown down. The Anointed One of God sits down to eat with tax-gatherers and sinners.

The divine interdependency

Yet this is no arrogant adolescent rebellion, no nervous defiance of tradition by one who is struggling to stand on his own feet. Christ's freedom is confident, relaxed and positive. It is so because he dares to go beyond independence to mature dependence. The Christ of the gospels is not one who "stands on his own feet", rather he rejoices to depend on the mystery of God he calls "Father". St. Luke's gospel shows Jesus at his baptism in Jordan praying. The heavens are opened, the Holy Spirit descends, the voice from heaven announces: "Thou art my beloved Son; with thee I am well pleased". Then we read that Jesus moves into his ministry "full of the Holy Spirit" (Luke 3:21 ff, 4:1). This is not a picture of rugged independence, of the autonomous hero. It is rather a picture of the freedom of mature dependence. St. John's gospel brings this out even more clearly. Here supremely Christ is the free one, the one who can dare to say: "I am the way, the truth and the life", and yet he is shown to be the one who draws such freedom from his very dependence on the Father: "I do not speak on my own authority; but the Father who dwells in me does his works" (John 14:6,10). "I have not spoken on my own authority", insists Jesus, "the Father who has sent me has himself given me commandment what to say and what to speak" (John 12:49).

Let us be clear, the relationship of the Son to the Father is not one of immature dependence. Jesus is no puppet manipulated by the deity. He utters the words of God but not as some inert public address system. He is not God's loudspeaker. It is "not by measure that" the Father has given the Spirit to the Son. "The Father loves the Son, and has given all things into his hand." The destiny of the world is entrusted to the Christ's freedom, the freedom that will battle in the Garden of Gethsemane, praying, yes really praying, that the cup of suffering will pass away and only through this struggle coming to the victorious "nevertheless, not my will but yours". Thus just as there is a dependence of the Son on the Father, so there is a dependence of the Father on the Son.

In fact what is here being revealed is the mystery of God as the life of joyful interdependence. The dialogue between Father and Son who are bound together by the bond of Holy Spirit which we see played out over those few years in Palestine is the enfleshment, the articulation in human terms, the "sacrament", of the divine love which is for all eternity. The doctrine of the Holy Trinity is not a piece of higher mathematical mystification, a speculation which is really marginal to the nitty gritty of Christian living. It is the articulation, in human words of course, of that deceptively simple affirmation that God is Love. The divine mystery is not just the outpouring, the giving of love, but also the return, the receiving of love. God is the joyful interdependence of love. The so-called "persons" of the Trinity are not "confused", they are not all the same. Each has his own identity. Each has, in this sense, the freedom to be "himself". And yet in this Trinity there is no before or after: no greater or less. "All three person are co-eternal together and co-equal". In the divine interdependence, liberty and equality are reconciled. Freedom to flourish exists for love.

Interdependency – not ideal but reality

We need to be clear what Christians are claiming in this trinitarian affirmation. This is no wild mystical speculation but a statement about ultimate reality. As we stretch out towards the vision of God we are not moving beyond this all too solid flesh into a sort of gaseous spirituality, into what is less real. God is that than which no greater can be conceived. The divine mystery is the most real, most solid. All of which is pointed to by those biblical images of God as the blazing fire and the strong mountain. What we are up against in God is reality so solid that we are overwhelmed. If we are then saying, in all seriousness that "God is the joyful interdependence of love" we are claiming that this "joyful interdependence" is what is most real. Politicians may say to us: "Ah, that may be a lovely dream, a beautiful vision but the 'real world' is about competition and power politics". We shall have to reply: "Granted that market forces and nuclear weapons are sober realities, what we are doing is not purveying some ideal which floats above all this, but insisting that beneath such sober realities lies the greater reality of the interdependence of love."

The Manchester school of economics set forth "competition as the law of the universe". That, said the nineteenth-century Anglican theologian F.D. Maurice, is "a lie". Politicians who stir uncomfortably at the implications of such theological orthodoxy are inclined to direct Christians back onto their knees. "Get on with your real business which is to pray." We are happy to do so, but the trouble is that it is precisely in our praying that we are driven up against the reality of this God. It is in our praying that our independence is undermined and we are thrust into the divine interdependence. Instead of having a man to man chat with the Great Pal, we find ourselves praying, often with unthinking and deceptive ease, "through Jesus Christ our Lord". Even to perform what seems the most politically inoccuous action of praying we find ourselves catapulted from "standing on our own feet" to being driven onto our knees to be carried by Jesus into the divine interdependence. "Because you are sons, God has sent the Spirit of his Son into our hearts, crying 'Abba! Father!' " (Galatians 4:6). "Likewise the Spirit helps us in our weakness; for we do not know how to pray as we ought, but the Spirit himself intercedes for us with sighs too deep for words" (Romans 8:26).

On the impossibility of standing on our own feet before God

There is no escape from this dependency which is at the heart of faith. It is the most important evangelical insight that we cannot parade before God on the basis of our moral or religious productivity. We are unprofitable servants — all of us and not just a class of failures to be classified as "sinners". The Apostle Paul is bleak about any illusions we may have:

> None is righteous, no, not one;
> no one understands, no one seeks for God.
> All have turned aside, together they have gone wrong;
> no one does good, not even one (Romans 3:9–11).

> "Nothing in my hands I bring,
> Simply to thy cross I cling."

Nothing is more fundamental to Christianity than this insight that we have not earned our standing before God, but that it is given to us as a gift of his mercy.

And by this continual gift, known to us as grace, we shall always live. Look again at the image of Christians as the "Body of Christ". In the Epistle to the Ephesians it is particularly used to emphasize our dependence on Christ the Head; ". . .we are to grow up in every way into him who is the head, into Christ, from whom the whole body, joined and knit together by every joint with which it is supplied, when each part is working properly, makes bodily growth and upbuilds itself in love" (Ephesians 4:15,16). So too the dependence of married love is seen as an image of the dependence of the Church on Christ (Ephesians 5:21ff). The same dependence is shown in the Johanine picture of the Vine and the branches. Jesus is the Vine and we are the branches: "Abide in me and I in you. As the branch cannot bear fruit by itself, unless it abides in the vine, neither can you, unless you abide in me" (John 15:1ff).

The dignity of depending on God

Yet this radical dependence is not to be immature dependence. The sinner kneeling before the Cross there affirms his dignity by accepting responsibility for his sin.

The disciple who must say "not I but the grace of God in me" is yet the one given the dignity of being a fellow-worker with Christ. This dependency is thus not in conflict with the call of the Epistle to the Galatians to equally radical freedom. We are sons and not slaves. As sons we are allowed to pray to the overwhelming mystery: "Abba, father". There is nothing grovelling and servile here. Indeed our discipleship means being "adopted" into the joyful interdependence of divine love.

Can we really talk of "interdependence"? Is not our relationship with God one of total dependence? Here the evangelical *sola gratia*, by grace alone, has to be filled out with the Catholic recognition that this grace is not only an acceptance of us as we are but also creative grace which does not leave us as we are. We really can share in the Son's free yes to the Father, we really can do the will of him who has sent us. Our little human "yes" does not manufacture the divine overflow of love. Even if we are planters and waterers, it is always God who gives the increase (1 Corinthians 3:5ff) but God depends on our "yes" to allow his love to make its way in the world. His creation involved the risk of love, for he has handed to us responsibility for the stewardship of this world. By our "yes" we can open the doors to life, by our "no" we can bring death and devastation. The reality of this interdependence is focused in the scene of the Annunciation. God, to achieve his saving incarnation, waits on the free "be it unto me according to thy word" of Mary.

Out of isolation into solidarity

Whatever may be said of other religions, the heart of the Christian gospel speaks not of isolated individualism but of interdependence, of communion. First and foremost that communion is with God: "our fellowship is with the Father and with his Son Jesus Christ" (1 John 1:3). To be baptized is to be plunged into solidarity with the divine. Yet this does not leave unaffected our relationship with other human beings. The same verse from I John which I have just quoted begins by saying: "that which we have seen and heard we proclaim also to you, so that you may have fellowship with us." Baptism is also a plunging into solidarity with our brothers and sisters in Christ.

The Christ who lives in the divine interdependence also lives by human interdependence. He is not a solitary. He gathers around him a circle of special followers and ensures that this is not a closed circle. He lives in solidarity with his fellow human beings, alert and sensitive to every need, taking responsibility for all who come his way. One characteristic of his ministry is that instead of living in the safe piety of the holy huddle, he goes out of his way to make the daily meal an occasion of welcome for tax-gatherers and sinners. Living in solidarity with the mystery of God does not pluck him from this world but drives him to the heart of its need. The way to his glory and fulfilment in God is simultaneously the way of ever deeper solidarity with humanity.

The binding of humanism to godliness

The Christ in fact is the one who binds godliness, with its thirst for solidarity with the divine, to humanism, with its longing for ever closer human solidarity. The old nightmare that we deprive this world of love by pouring it out on the skies is dispelled. The twofold commandment "to love God and to love one's neighbour as oneself", proves not to be twofold in the sense of generating an inevitable conflict as we struggle to apportion the proper amount of "love" to each obligation. The way to being human is the way to God. To those who care for the hungry and needy, God will say: "I say to you, as you did it to the least of my brethren, you did it to me" (Matthew 25:40). "Beloved let us love one another; for love is of God, and he who loves is born of God and knows God. He who does not love does not know God; for God is love" (1 John 4:7,8).

The Christian community lives to make incarnate the divine interdependence through human interdependence. The aim of freedom is to serve one another in love. It means taking responsibility for the other person, living as those who know they are "members one of another". This involves the sort of sensitivity to the other which leads us to "weep with those who weep and rejoice with those who rejoice". But it also involves the practical structuring of this responsibility. Our commitment to human solidarity will not be measured simply by fine feelings. St. Luke provides a, possibly idealized, picture of such practical solidarity in the primitive sharing of goods: "All who believed were together and had all things in common; and they sold their possessions and goods and distributed them to all, as any had need" (Acts 2:44). But the same sense of responsibility is shown in St. Paul's careful attention to the provision of famine relief by the better-off communities for the poorer churches of Judaea.

The sacrificial meal of solidarity

Yet this sense of human solidarity is not simply to do with the good works which the believing community performs. I am to take responsibility for my neighbour on the material level because it is at the spiritual level that I discover this interdependence. The Lord who tells me to pray, tells me to pray out of a sense of solidarity, to pray "*Our* Father". The heart of our worship is not solitary prayer but that communal celebration of the Eucharist in which "we who are many are one body, for we all partake of the same loaf" (1 Corinthians 10:17). Here is the place of "communion" which, because it is communion with the mystery of love, is also communion with our brothers and sisters. It is the Liturgy – literally the work (*ergon*) of the people (*laos*). So that we are to think of this as a truly communal celebration, not with the priest doing something for us, but with all of us doing something together, each performing his or her proper role. The fact that we depend on having a priest for there to be a Mass, does not trouble us if we have grasped this doctrine of interdependence. Like the paralysed man in the gospels, we are happy to depend on another, happy to be carried into the presence of the Lord by someone else. That, for us, is the name of the human game – always being carried by other people. In the case of our dependence on the priest for the Mass, we are also articulating our total dependence, not simply on this priest, but on him as a sign or pointer to Christ. No priest, no Mass is meant to show that the Eucharist cannot be manufactured by the community, but comes "from above", that is from Christ. It is the place where our dependence on a human being most clearly points us to our ultimate dependence on God.

People sometimes imagine there is a conflict between the Mass as the sacrament of the Lord's sacrifice and as the communal meal of Christians. The conflict is illusory, for the Mass is the very centre of human communion precisely because it focuses on Calvary the very centre of God's costly communion with humanity. It is God's solidarity with us, going right down into our depths, which can create that real human solidarity rooted in the radical solidarity of God with us on Calvary.

Breadth and depth of solidarity

Through the liturgy we discover too the breadth of this solidarity. We stand not only shoulder to shoulder with the sniffling, coughing congregation around us but "with the whole host of heaven." This is the *communion* which leaps the barrier of death, a solidarity from which none, not even the dead, are excluded save through a determination to be excluded. It is because of this solidarity in the love of God – "whether we live or whether we die, we are the Lord's" – that Catholics are liberated both to pray for the dead and to request the dead to pray for them. We are not taking out celestial insurance policies or becoming engaged in rescue operations beyond the grave; all this loving commerce between heaven and earth is a simple expression of how seriously we take the breadth of human solidarity. Just as we know we must be catholic in leaping over barriers of class, colour and nationality, so too we must be catholic in leaping this last barrier of death. If Christ be risen and interdependence be the name of the human game, why should not the dead be glad that our loving prayers continue?

And so one could go on showing how the most intimate and deeply personal practices of faith have also an accompanying sense of twofold solidarity – with God and with one's fellows. Personal religion, personal prayer is not lonely religion or lonely prayer. For Catholics this can be seen most clearly in the sacrament of reconciliation. As I have already said it is here in confession of particular sin that we most affirm that we are free and responsible people – but it is also here that we recognize that our offence is not "just" a matter between the individual and God, here we recognize that our sin injures the community. It is therefore right that I confess my sin to the representative of the community and that the forgiveness of God is communicated to me through this same representative. The gospel of human interdependence is not simply some adjunct of faith called "social teaching" nor some hobby for Christians with a political bent, but it is at the very centre of worship and spirituality that the contradiction between the personal and the communal is denied. Right here the affirmation is made and lived out that no one is an island, that to be human is to grasp the interdependence into which we were born.

Individual and community – tensions and conflicts

To deny this contradiction does not mean to deny the conflicts which can arise between the individual and the community. If one is really serious about the business of fostering human giftedness, if one is saying to the arm and the leg; "Be yourself in order to enrich the body", then there is always the risk of conflict. The temptation of the community is, of course, to rein in this giftedness, to control it, subdue it, tame it – for, it is perceived, if individuality gets out of hand the body will come to pieces. There is thus a built-in tension between the claims of unity, holding the show together, and the claims of catholicity, taking on board as much giftedness as you can seize. How can the city at once have walls strong enough to preserve its distinctive common life while keeping its gates open wide enough to embrace the further enrichment of that life?

As Christianity emerges from the womb of Judaism it necessarily moves into rough and threatening waters. This going out again and again involves meeting new cultures, new ways of thinking, new raw material of human flourishing – and in this are both risk and the possibility of enrichment. Because the risks are real the temptation is either to stand still or to retreat back into the womb. Catholicism is in business to take the risk and to go boldly for enrichment.

In conflict armed with love or with institution?

With what is the Christian enterprise armed as it takes this risk? It can only be armed with the same armour which its Lord wore in his conflict, that is, the armour of love. For it is love which binds all together, love as the goal which preserves us from the destructiveness of using our giftedness for self-aggrandizement rather than the common good. So it is that Paul, having urged us to allow human giftedness to flourish, reminds us that the best gift to covet is that of love, without which we are noisy gongs and clanging cymbals (1 Corinthians 13). But have Christians just trusted in the armour of love to reconcile individual and community? Have they not, in fact, put more trust in the armour of authority and structure? Even Paul seems to have denied his own insight by retreating to the laying down of law and the appeal to apostolic authority.

83

Here we come across the old conflict between spirit and institution. Is the history of Christianity one of a fall from trust in love to a reliance on authority and structures? Certainly it did not take long for the latter to emerge. Although the New Testament evidence shows a variety of patterns of organization, organization there is, and in the Pastoral Epistles it shows some signs of hardening into a unified pattern. Certainly, within a few hundred years, there was established such a pattern, complete with bishops – (including a leading bishop who presided "in love" at Rome), priests and deacons. The question is: "Is this a fall from trust in love, or a valid organizational embodiment of love?" This which seems a rather remote ecclesiastical debate, actually touches upon a real issue which confronts every body politic: "Should you leave the bond of the common life to be woven from the charity of individuals, or are there structures which can at least help or hinder the holding together in unity of flourishing human giftedness?"

Now I certainly do not want to dodge the facts of the oppressiveness of Christian institutions. Too much blood has been spilt to allow such evasion – too much giftedness inhibited or crushed in the name of the common good, yet I have to say such oppression cannot always be laid at the door of "organization men. As often it has come from men of the Spirit, the charismatics, individuals with burning conviction who have tended to narrow the Church to the confines of their particular vision. Wild desert monks, martyrs' fan clubs, fierce denouncers of popes and bishops, lay leaders of churches which have rejected all priests and ministers – these have been as tyrannical and authoritarian as any institutional men. Organized religion may be denounced – and often with good reason. However, the track record of disorganized religion is not that reassuring.

The binding together of spirit and institution

The thrust of Christian faith is precisely to bind together

spirit and institution for this is the faith which hinges on incarnation – God who is spirit, the eternal one who cannot be confined by time and space, taking our fleshly human nature and using this to express his life. Because embodiment is no decline from spirituality, it becomes part and parcel of the whole Christian life. Although we are always being enticed beyond, made to stretch out towards the transcendent, we believe that the transcendent touches us through a network of signs and symbols. As the poet Edwin Muir insists, it is a falling away from faith when the Word made flesh is reduced to word again.

What is made explicit in the incarnation and the consequent sacrementalism of the Church, is of course implicit in our understanding of creation. The barrier to the divine is here not the material, the physical, the thing-like – for God, surveying his creation, has said: "Behold it is very good." The barrier is set up not by the flesh, but by sin, which is at heart the denial or rebellion of spirit. It is Adam in his full dignity as man, Adam aspiring to be "god", who falls. It is not flesh and organization of the flesh in human structures which is inherently sinful, but what spirit does with these things; indeed it is just at the point where we wind ourselves too high that we are most likely to fall.

Authority – heart of the institutional problem

The heart of the problem of the "institution" is the problem of authority. If what ultimately binds us together is the holy Spirit of love, then what need have we for external authority? Certainly a tension between the external and the internal is perceived in the very pages of the New Testament. The Johanine writings are, by and large, inimicable to external authority. If the role of Peter, as leader, is exalted in John 21, we are reminded that this has to be a service of love, marked by such a deep commitment to the Lord, that he lays down his life, and we are pointed to the different role of the mysterious "beloved disciple" who must serve the Lord in his own way. We are never allowed to forget that it was this disciple who got to the tomb first and who first believed. Similarly the first letter of John is addressed to those who, far from having the truth imposed on them from outside by some external authority, "have been anointed by the holy one" and thus know the truth from within (1 John 2:20).

Yet with all this, the figure of Peter remains, called to "feed the lambs" to "tend the sheep" (John 21:15–20). What we have to absorb from this Johanine witness, which accepts the leadership role of Peter alongside its suspicion of the structured Church, is the ambiguity of all structure and authority. It will never be an unalloyed good. The fundamental word on the exercise of authority remains that of the Lord: "You know that those who are supposed to rule over the Gentiles lord it over them, and their great men exercise authority over them. But it shall not be so among you; but whoever would be great among you must be your servants" (Mark 10:42–43). In line with this, the instruction to the presbyters in 1 Peter 5:2–3 is "to tend the flock of God . . . not as domineering over those in your charge but being examples to the flock."

The question-mark over authority

Our age has every right to sniff with suspicion at authority from whatever quarter it comes, and perhaps the more it is clad in the vestments of faith, the more suspicious it should be. We have seen too much cruelty in its abuse ever again to yield uncritically to its commands. In the name of obedience and submission to lawful authority terrible crimes have been committed. The plea that I was simply "obeying orders" is now seen for what it is – an abandonment of human responsibility in the face of demands which no human organization should make. This is once again the flight into immature dependence, a rejection of my human dignity. Every exercise of authority has now a question mark hanging over it: "Is this the sort of authority behind which people hide? Is this the sort of authority which fosters a state of immature dependence? Does it fashion robots rather than free persons?"

Authority as service of the common good

But this recognition of the ambiguity of authority, of the moral need of a post-Nuremberg generation to probe its credentials, does not consign it to the dustbin. Despite dark shadows, we need to think calmly about authority, for it is surely a necessary service and, the more complex and ambitious we make our human enterprises, the more necessary this service must be. It is not simply because human life is "nasty and brutish", that restraints have to be placed upon our appetites. It is not just that "every man", being so energetically for "himself", has to be prevented from trampling on his neighbour. It is rather the richer, the more varied and exciting the common enterprise is, the more some control is needed and it is so needed, not just for the sake of restraint, but of achieving this grand and complex purpose. While human weaknesses give good reason for having authority, John Finnis insists that:

> . . .more interestingly, it is also true that the greater the intelligence and skill of a group's members, and the greater their commitment and dedication to common purposes and common good, the more authority and regulation may be required, to enable that group to achieve its common purpose, common good.

Authority as referee or conductor

Of course the case for authority rests upon establishing the case for the "common good". If we are simply individualists, rejecting any notion of "society", then we shall see only a negative role for authority, the restraint of individual excesses. Take the question of sport. A certain number of activities can be enjoyed by the individual. He can run by himself, even have a round of golf by himself. But the excitement may be said to begin when the individual becomes involved in a game with others. Once we are into games we are also into rules and referees. The whole thing, just because it is a more interesting and complex activity, needs authority. Here literally the lines of the pitch have to be drawn and control has to be exercised. For the game to work, the participants need to accept that judgements have to be made and that the referee's decision is final. This is no grovelling before arbitrary authority, for the referee is only there to serve the playing of the game. If he is one of those nervous referees, trying to assert his authority, the whistle will be for ever blowing, and the game will not be allowed to flow forward. There is an art in exercising this sort of authority – to be in control and yet to ensure that this control enables the game to take place. Successful authority on the field knows as much how to play the "advantage rule" and let things carry on, as how firmly to restrain when things get out of hand.

Another model of such creative authority is that of the conductor of the orchestra. To be a gifted soloist is a very good thing, but to be part of the common enterprise of an orchestra is also a very good thing. Orchestral playing is a richer and more complex operation and therefore needs its conductor. The soloist needs no conductor, even the modest quartet needs no conductor, but the particular good of orchestral playing does. The conductor exercises authority. His say goes. He will impose his interpretation on this particular piece of music. Yet without musicians he is nothing. His skill is to weave together all these individual skills, to fashion them into a common enterprise. His authority is real but it is at the service of the orchestra. Sometimes he will need to restrain the too-vigorous brass section while at other times he will need to bring forward a reticent woodwind section. To conduct is not just to repress – it is supremely to bring out the best, to achieve the best possible performance.

A *mature acceptance of authority*

Such a positive view of authority, as a service which liberates individuals for the common enterprise, is necessary if we are to think maturely about authority in Church and state. We need such a view if we are to escape from those forms of authority which foster immaturity, and if we are to advance beyond the scarcely less immature rejection of all forms of authority. Christianity has been and still is haunted by problems of this nature. Authority is, for very good and understandable reasons, struggled with and rejected; but then it becomes apparent that, without it, the common enterprise is threatened, so it makes a come-back in equally unacceptable forms. While an authority, unexposed to criticism, generates rebellion, the free-for-all which results from the rebellion is equally uncritical of its own individualism, and so prepares the conditions for a flight back to authority. Despite manifest failures to handle this problem creatively, we can at least claim that Christians are busy working at it and that this work could have consequences for society at large. Christianity contains within itself, both in the Johanine suspicion of structure and in her Lord's condemnation of pagan models of authority, a perpetual critique of its exercise.

Authority and conscience

But this is a way of testing valid authority, not of abolishing it. Many Christians of course think the authority of God, which they still by and large accept, cannot be mediated through the flesh of institutions. If it is present at all, it is considered to be present only to the individual conscience. Now certainly I would want to insist that the individual conscience is the only mechanism free responsible persons have for receiving divine truth. This has traditionally been expressed in the dictum that every individual has an absolute duty to follow his own conscience. But this does *not* mean that conscience is infallible. It is to be followed because it is the only "receiver" we have; yet it can objectively be mistaken. Which is why the tradition not only tells me to follow my conscience *but also* that I have the duty to make sure my conscience is "informed" or educated. For conscience is not a divine "bit" in me – it is just "me", as a complete person with mind as well as heart, deciding what is to be done.

The formation, the shaping of this "me", with the provision of adequate and true information, is thus decisive for the proper operation of the judgements of what we call "conscience". The insistence that, if asked to raise my glass to ecclesiastical authority, I shall first raise it to conscience does *not* mean the denigration of authority. If my conscience is to be informed then the best information available is of ultimate, that is divine truth. This truth does not simply bubble up from within. It confronts me from outside. It stands as a tough and towering rock before me. Moreover it does not come at me neat and naked. Because I am incurable flesh and blood, it must come to me via such flesh and blood. In other words to expose myself to the truth of God, I cannot just gaze into the skies or shout up the chimney for an answer, I must expect that it will be mediated through flesh and blood like mine. Supremely this will be through the flesh and blood of Jesus of Nazareth but, in terms of Christian faith, this will be through him, not as a dead and distant memory whose influence is now reduced to the written word, but through him alive and present speaking through that flesh and blood of his which belongs to the members of his body, the Church.

Authority as the enabling of individual giftedness

The aim of authority is to embody what St. Paul was after in chapters 12 and 13 of 1 Corinthians – that is, the flourishing of individual giftedness in all its amazing variety so that this flourishing brings, not self-aggrandizement and the division inevitable in the clash of thus inflated selves, but enrichment of the common life. Authority in the Christian Church does not simply pass orders down the line, it should act far more under the image of the conductor who exercises a real authority but does so to employ this variety of gifted individual musicians in the common enterprise of orchestral music. One of the earliest witnesses to the development of apostolic authority in the Church is St. Ignatius of Antioch. As he wrote of the duty of obedience to the bishop he articulated that duty in similar terms:

> . . . it is fitting that you should live in harmony with the will of the bishop, as indeed you do. For your justly famous presbytery, worthy of God, is attuned to the bishop as the strings to the harp. Therefore by your concord and harmonious love Jesus Christ is sung. Now do each of you join in this choir, that being harmoniously in concord you may receive the key of God in unison and sing with one voice through Jesus Christ to the Father . . ."[1]

What our faith is saying is that there is more to life than being a gifted soloist, that there is the further "common" good, the symphony to which we are able to bring our individual gifts. The service of authority exists, not to crush these gifts, but precisely to bring them together for this purpose. Authority exists for the task of reconciling preciously rugged individuality with the common life of interdependence.[2]

Interdependence and political structure

This Christian experience of authority and institution can be of value as we reflect on the limitations and yet necessity of political structures in generating the common good of interdependence. Of course laws cannot make us more

91

charitable or brotherly. And laws should not get us off the hook of personal responsibility. Yet we cannot proceed along the lines of spirit/institution divide, as if the task of being members one of another should be left to individual initiative with the institution simply holding the ring by offering to individuals the greatest possible freedom. It is not quite enough for the state to create the best conditions for wealth creation, leaving its distribution to individual decision. Partly this is because there are some tasks which are beyond the individual and require organized joint action. But, more significantly, political arrangement for good or ill spells out a message of what this society believes to be the desirable life. Laws and institutions set before us social goals.

This is clearly understood by conviction politicians of the new right. They have legislated to clip the wings of trade unions, to prune some welfare benefits, and introduce the poll tax in place of domestic rates. These institutional actions have been taken in the belief that they would help generate a more bracing social atmosphere which would elicit the desired objectives of more individual enterprise, initiative and responsibility. If political arrangements can assist such goals, why should not different political arrangements assist different political goals? The spirit of interdependence requires the bones of structure. That, at least, I suggest is what Christian experience, of a quite painful variety, leads us to recognize.

Notes

1. Ignatius, *To the Ephesians* 4.
2. See Hans Urs von Balthasar, *Truth is Symphonic – Aspects of Christian Pluralism,* Ignatius Press 1987.

FIVE

THE UNIFIED
VISION – AN EXAMPLE

I have argued that Christians have a distinct vision of humanity in which the unique giftedness and freedom of the individual is affirmed along with our essentially social nature. I have suggested that a society which finds unsatisfactory the images of both a dependency culture with its all-embracing state and that of an independency culture with its offer of ladders to individual achievement feels after such an image of interdependence. This Christian contribution is not just some wild theoretical dream, it has a claim on our attention because it is the fruit of hard wrestling and painful practise. Moreover the vision which it holds out to the world is not some quirk of pale pink clerics who have lost interest in real religion but something which proceeds from the very heart of orthodox traditional faith. There is not a fundamental gospel with a "social gospel" tagged on as an extra. The vision which faith offers is a coherent one which embraces both prayer and politics.

The need for a coherent vision

In order to underline this coherence I want to give as an example the teaching of one man, Pope Paul II. Whatever critics may accuse the present Pope of being, few would be found to call him a pale pink trendy cleric. But then such is the continuing force of ecclesiastical prejudice that others will find popery more off-putting than pinkery. I have chosen to focus on the Pope's teaching partly, of course, because as a Roman Catholic I have a particular respect for his teaching office, but also because his views do not stand by themselves but are quite explicitly a contribution to the development of a particular tradition of Christian thinking about society. Given time I could as well try to explicate that Anglican tradition of social thinking which stretches from the nineteenth-century F.D. Maurice, through Bishop Charles Gore and Archbishop William Temple, and through the more colourful Stewart Headlam and Conrad Noel to the recent Archbishops' Commission *Faith in the City*. This is I believe has a similar coherence, in the sense that reflection on the City of Man springs from the liveliest convictions about the transcendent reality of the City of God. The heroes of this Anglican tradition are men of politics because they are men of prayer.

However, in recent times Pope John Paul II has been the most notable exponent of a view of society in which both the dignity of the individual person and the virtue of human solidarity have been emphasized. Liberty and Fraternity have been brought together in his teaching. It is one of the tragedies of ecclesiastical polemic that this unified vision has not come across to the general public. Fragments of his teaching, normally about sex, have, for propaganda purposes, been lifted out of context and the Pope has been made to appear simply the hammer of liberal Western permissiveness. Anyone who has actually studied the text of his encyclicals and speeches will find nothing as trite and pedestrian as this. Complex, even tortuous, though his thinking and writing may sometimes appear to be, all is in the interests of an exploration of that rich Christian humanism which was the theme of his first encyclical *Redemptor Hominis*. There he claimed that "the primary route that the Church must travel" . . . is "Man in the full truth of his existence, of his personal being and also of his community and social being" for this is "the way traced out by Christ himself, the way that leads invariably through the mystery of the Incarnation and the Redemption."[1]

There is a time for gathering and a time for scattering. One age will be impressed or depressed by the solid unified front which Catholicism presents to the world. The next age will see this front in disarray, its neatly woven coherence unpicked by a hundred and one critical unravellers. Such times of scattering are necessary, for faith can become to smooth, too sleek for its true health; its very cohesion can be will-nigh idolatrous. Yet faith cannot live on the thin gruel of criticism and Pope John Paul has surely been right to attempt once again to construct a unified Christian vision. He is above all a missionary and thus works to show that the Church's social teaching is not an optional extra or a hobby for a few enthusiasts but part and parcel of the total message, a moral imperative rooted in our understanding of God and the ways of God. So instead of reaching into a rag-bag of Catholic "awkwardnesses" on such issues as abortion, birth control and euthanasia, the Pope presents a consistent pro-life message which stretches from the unborn to the elderly and handicapped. It brings together the so-called "right to life" and the issues of justice and peace, in what American bishops have called "a seamless robe".

Developing a tradition – continuity and novelty

Although the Pope is personally a great apostle of such a unified vision, he is always conscious of being the servant and articulator of a tradition. He is not just having bright ideas of his own but communicating the message of a community. So in writing his encyclical on "Social Concern" (*Sollicitudo Rei Socialis* 1988), the Pope explicitly states that he is contributing to a tradition first articulated by Leo XIII in 1891 (*Rerum Novarum*) and continued by Pius XI (*Quadragesimo Anno* 1931), John XXIII (*Mater et Magistra* 1961) and Paul VI (*Populorum Progressio* 1967). This tradition, John Paul II states, "builds up gradually, as the

Church in the fullness of the word revealed by Christ Jesus and with the assistance of the Holy Spirit reads events as they unfold in the course of history".[2]

There are thus two aspects to the development of this tradition. Its relation to the fundamentals of the gospel and its relation to the world through which this gospel moves:

> On the one hand it is *constant*, for it remains identical in its fundamental inspiration, in its "principles of reflection", in its "criteria of judgement", in "its basic directives for action", and above all in its vital link with the Gospel of the Lord. On the other hand, it is for ever *new*, because it is subject to the necessary and opportune adaptations suggested by the changes in historical conditions and by the unceasing flow of the events which are the setting of the life of people and society.[3]

This means that the Church cannot just reach down from a shelf some handbook which contains instructions for any and every age. In the words of the Vatican II document on "the Church and the Modern World" ('*Gaudium et Spes*'), it has to "scrutinize the signs of the times and to interpret them in the light of the Gospel."[4] Christian insight about society comes both from a reflection on fundamental faith and a reflection on what is going on in the world around us. It is this dialogue between faith and the facts of life which constitutes the particular contribution of Vatican II. Thus John Paul II's avowed aim is to engage in a "theological investigation of the present world". What he investigates is what every political commentator and journalist investigates – the bare facts are the same for all – but the aim and object of the exercise is different from that of other commentators. Like the Old Testament prophets, the Church is in business to discern in all these facts the hand and the imperative of God.

Commitment to human concerns – shades and light

Vatican II's Constitution "On the Church in the Modern World" begins by announcing the Christian commitment to the world.

> The joy and hope, the grief and anguish of the men of our time, especially of those who are poor or afflicted in any way, are the joy and hope, the grief and anguish of the followers of Christ as well. Nothing that is genuinely human fails to find an echo in their hearts. [5]

It is important to notice that this sense of "solidarity with the human race" contains both hope and grief. Some have criticized the Council document for being tainted by sixties euphoria. However much enthusiasts may have plucked from the document the theme of hope and neglected that of grief and have thus given an unbalanced interpretation of it, the document itself avoids the pitfalls of both optimism and pessimism.

Pope John Paul retains this balance in his encyclical on Social Concern. His survey of the contemporary world faces the fact that the high hopes of twenty years ago have not been realized. There is a widening gulf between the affluent North and the poverty-stricken South. The housing crisis and unemployment are noted. The crippling effect of servicing of debt by poor nations is underlined. The conflict between the liberal capitalist culture of the West and the marxist collectivist one of the East has not only drained valuable resources into armaments programmes but has been exported to precisely those impoverished parts of the world which can least afford such ideological luxuries.

And yet together with this grief and anguish, positive aspects of the modern world are emphasized – a new concern for human rights, articulated in the United Nations declaration, a growing recognition of the radical interdependence of the human race, a realization that peace and justice are indivisible, that we cannot enjoy the delights of the former where injustice generates the very conflicts which threaten it, a concern for the environment, a new sensitivity to the delicate fabric of this one world of which we humans are but part. As well as pinpointing such signs of hope, the Pope pays a proper and often neglected tribute to "the generous commitment of statesmen, politicians, economists, trade unionists, people of science and international officials . . . who at no small personal sacrifice try to resolve the world's ills".[6]

The moral centre

Reading the "signs of the times", the Pope is neither an euphoric optimist nor a gloomy pessimist. He witnesses to that authentic Christian realism which faces the fact of evil and yet sees that the work of the Creator, if defaced by sin, is not destroyed. "Development is not a straightforward process, as it were automatic and in itself limitless, as though, given certain conditions, the human race were able to progress rapidly towards an undefined perfection of some kind."[7] Such "naive mechanistic optimism has been replaced by a well-founded anxiety for the fate of humanity." "The main obstacles to development will be overcome only by means of *essentially moral decisions*".[8] This insistence that our human problems are basically not technical but moral is a manifestation of the Pope's belief in the dignity of the human person. Way back in *Redemptor Hominis* he saw the human race afflicted by the fear of people becoming just means to an end, the fear that the extraordinary power we had achieved might be turned upon ourselves. "Does progress", he asked, "make human life on earth 'more human'?" In face of such fear of becoming just a "thing" ground down by forces we cannot control, John Paul II affirmed the dignity of the person called to share in the "kingly function of Christ himself":

The essential meaning of this "kingship" and "dominion"

of man over the visible world, which the Creator himself gave man for his task, consists in the priority of ethics over technology, in the primacy of the person over things, and in the superiority of spirit over matter. [9]

Primacy of the person

This insistence on the "primacy of the person" brings us to the Pope's characteristic personalism. He is not interested in some windy abstraction called "humanity" or "the human race" but in each unique individual. Typically, when facing the economic problem of the indebtedness of Third World countries, he sees it in human personal terms. "Is it merely a rhetorical question to ask how many infants and children die every day in Africa because resources are being swallowed up in debt repayment?" This is deeply rooted in his theology. The marvel of the incarnation is that "God entered the history of humanity and, as a man became an actor in that history, one of the thousands of millions of human beings but at the same time Unique!" [10] By assuming the particularity of being a human being, "he, the Son of God, in a certain way united himself with each man." [11]

The Pope never loses sight of the dignity and responsibility of the individual. This comes out in his consistent evangelical teaching on the importance of personal conversion. There can be no evasion of this by trying to lose ourselves in the collective, not even in the divine community. "Conversion is a particularly profound inward act in which the individual cannot be replaced by others and cannot make the community be a substitute for him." [12] In observing the practise of individual confession "the Church is . . . defending the human soul's individual right: man's right to a more personal encounter with the crucified forgiving Christ".

Human rights and freedom

The Pope is thus an ardent advocate of human rights and freedom. He is more definite than any other pope in advocating democratic forms of government, those which allow the "free and responsible participation" of citizens. "It is important that as far as possible the developing nations . . . should favour the self-affirmation of each citizen."[13] While

> other nations need to reform certain unjust structures, and in particular their political institutions, in order to replace corrupt, dictatorial and authoritarian forms of government by democratic and participatory ones . . . For the health of a political community – as expressed in the free and responsible participation of all citizens in public affairs, in the rule of law and in respect for and promotion of human rights – is the necessary condition and sure guarantee of the development "of the whole individual and of all people."

Because it is important that societies should encourage the freedom of individuals to flourish and use their giftedness, the Pope is critical of the suppression of "the right of economic initiative". The denial of this right "in the name of an alleged 'equality' of everyone in society, diminishes the spirit of initiative. . . . As a consequence, there arises, not so much a true equality as a 'levelling down' ". The result of thus repressing human giftedness is to produce a dependency culture:

> In the place of creative initiative there appears passivity, dependence and submission to the bureaucratic apparatus which, as the only "ordering" and "decision-making" body – if not also the "owner" – of the entire totality of goods and means of production, puts everyone in a position of almost absolute dependence, which is similar to the traditional dependence of the worker-proletarian in

capitalism. This provokes a sense of frustration or desperation and predisposes people to opt out of national life, impelling many to emigrate and also favouring a form of 'psychological' emigration.[14]

Clearly Pope John Paul's experience of marxist collectivism in Poland gives this description its particular edge but it can, with justice, be seen as a warning to democratic socialist societies of the dangers of dependency cultures.

The false freedom of consumerism

Such a stress on individual freedom to flourish does not lead the Pope into an euphoric celebration of the "market economy". For him freedom is not freedom simply to do as I please. He has some very sharp things to say about the way "superdevelopment" undermines genuine human freedom. "This superdevelopment, which consists in an excessive availability of every kind of material goods for the benefit of certain social groups, easily makes people slaves of 'possession'."

Such "consumerism" undermines freedom because it is located in "having" rather than in "being". Not that "having" as such is wrong, but our "having" has to be directed to some higher goal. Mere acquisition of "goods" is not enough. "Goods" have to be subordinated to man's "being", that is, to his true vocation. In other words: "Does the possession of this thing help or hinder me from becoming that true and unique human being which God would have me be? 'Do my goods make me more or less human?' " Again the Pope here draws on his Polish experience: granted that marxist collectivism has suppressed human giftedness and flourishing, do we really want to plunge out of this "frying-pan" into the fire of Western economic liberal capitalism?

Here is surely one of the increasingly sharp questions of our age. The slogan may read: "Not Karl Marx but Marks and Spencers!" – but the attitude of many in the Eastern bloc is that articulated by this Polish Pope which perhaps can be summed up like this: "What we seek is neither domination by the collective nor by market forces. We want simply to be human beings who can flourish and be ourselves – not just for our own sakes but also for the sake of the common good." It is both simplistic and euphoric of Margaret Thatcher to interpret what is going on in Eastern Europe as a pure conversion to the joys of the market. Certainly the market has shown itself to be a more efficient mechanism than that of bureaucratic state centralism in the business of wealth creation, but this leaves the further question unanswered: To what uses shall we put this wealth? Conversion to the market as mechanism is not the same as conversion to the market as some mysterious god-like providence.

Humanity as community and social being

Pope John Paul focuses on the unique value of the person yet is not an individualist. Everyone for himself choosing his own self-appointed goals and values is not his creed. "The obligation to commit oneself to the development of peoples is not just an individual duty, and still less an individualistic one, as if it were possible to achieve this development through the isolated efforts of each individual."[15] The "full truth" of the existence of humanity is, not only "personal being" but also "community and social being".[16] The Pope believes in such a thing as "the common good", believes that "society" exists. He is thus as sharply critical of liberal capitalism as he is of marxist collectivism. He denounces: ". . . the existence of economic, financial and social mechanisms which, although they are manipulated by people, often function almost automatically, thus accentuating the situation of wealth for some and poverty for the rest."[17] The operation of "market forces" thus operates against the good of the Third World: ". . . the debtor nations, in order to service their debt, find themselves obliged to export capital needed for improving, or at least maintaining their standard of living."[18]

The solidarity of free persons

In place of the marxist collectivism, which denies human giftedness, freedom and initiative, and in place of the free for all of the market which both increases the gulf between rich and poor and brings the new slavery to consumerism, the Pope offers the goal of the human solidarity of free persons. This goal is sternly realistic in that it responds better than marxism or capitalism to the fact of our growing human interdependence. It is an ethical imperative to meet our growing awareness of inhabiting one small world. To seek this goal requires nothing less than a conversion but: "On the path towards the desired conversion, towards the overcoming of the moral obstacles to development, it is already possible to point to the positive and moral value of the growing awareness of '*interdependence*' among individuals and nations."

When this sense of interdependence as a fact of life is seen as "a system determining relationships in the contemporary world" then the proper response is "*solidarity*".

> This . . . is not a feeling of vague compassion or shallow distress at the misfortunes of so many people, both near and far. On the contrary, it is a firm and persevering determination to commit oneself to the common good; that is to say to the good of all and of each individual, because we are all really responsible for all.[19]

This model of "human solidarity" avoids the impersonalism of the collective for the exercise of this virtue

> within each society is valid when its members recognize one another as persons. Those who are influential, because they have a greater share of goods and common services, should feel responsible for the weaker and be

ready to share with them all they possess. Those who are weaker, for their part, in the same spirit of solidarity, should not adopt a purely passive attitude or one that is destructive of the social fabric, but, while claiming their legitimate rights, should do what they can for the good of all.[20]

"Both peoples and individuals must enjoy. . . . fundamental equality". This is not based on an attempt to reduce people to a dull grey sameness but on "a lively awareness of the value of the rights of all and each person".[21] The Pope is pointing towards a goal which lies beyond both immature dependency and anti-social independence. "Solidarity helps us to see the 'other' – whether a person, people or nation – not just as some kind of instrument. . . . but as our 'neighbour', a 'helper'."[22] It is characterized not by the pursuit of private goals but by a sense of responsibility for our neighbour.

Private property and the universal destination of goods

The possession of private property, good in itself as an instrument of personal flourishing and identity, must be informed by the principle that the goods of creation are meant for all. This principle of "the universal destination of earthly goods" is spelt our very clearly by Vatican II: I cannot consider myself to be the absolute owner of my goods. I cannot do what I like with my own for in truth I am only the steward of these goods. "In his use of things man should regard the external goods he legitimately owns not merely as exclusive to himself but common to others also, in the sense that they can benefit others as well as himself."[23]

All this, of course, is building on the teaching of St. Thomas Aquinas. He defends the principle of private property on the grounds that this enhances the sense of personal responsibility. We take more care with what is our own. However this does not undermine the more fundamental principle that "the earth is the Lord's". So, in answering the question "Whether it is lawful to steal through stress of need?" Thomas answers:

> Things which are of human right cannot derogate from natural right or Divine right. Now according to the natural order established by divine providence, inferior things are ordained for the purpose of succouring man's need by their means. Wherefore the division and appropriation of things which are based on human law, do not preclude the fact that man's needs have to be remedied by means of these very things. Hence whatever certain people have in superabundance is due, by natural law, to the purpose of succouring the poor. [24]

This is but the application of human solidarity, the common good, to our possession of riches. All that I own has to be treated with a sense of responsibility for my neighbours, not just as a matter of private charity, but as one of natural justice.

The theological anchorage of human solidarity

This notion of solidarity much favoured and developed by the present Pope is not his own invention, to be treated as a peculiar Polish export. Vatican II gives us its theological foundation in the section "The Word made Flesh and Human Solidarity". [25] Here we are reminded that "God did not create men to live as individuals but to come together in the formation of social unity." The instruments of his salvation are not solitaries but the people of Israel and the new Israel of the Church. Indeed "the communitarian character (of God's work) is perfected and fulfilled in the work of Jesus Christ, for the Word made flesh willed to share in human fellowship". It is he who sets up the Church to be "a sacrament and sign of the unity of the human race". Pope John Paul also makes clear the deep theological anchorage of solidarity:

beyond human and natural bonds . . . there is discerned in the light of faith a new model of the unity of the human race, which must ultimately inspire our solidarity. This supreme model of unity, which is a reflection of the intimate life of God, one God in three Persons, is what we Christians mean by the word "communion". This specifically Christian communion, . . . is the soul of the Church's vocation to be a "sacrament". [26]

The tension and loose ends of a developing tradition – the structures of sin

We have to be clear that the Pope is making his contribution to a tradition which is always struggling to articulate a unified vision of the person in society. This means that there are lines of development to be traced in the Pope's own thinking, that there are certain unresolved tensions and some loose ends. But this is precisely what we would expect from a genuine dialogue between the enduring gospel and the ever changing conditions of the human scene.

Take for instance John Paul's thinking on "the structures of sin". Should the ills of our world all be blamed on personal moral failures, or is there some way in which the impersonal organizations of society become almost "sacraments" of sin? There is a whole theology in the New Testament of how Christ liberates humanity, not simply from individual sinfulness, but also from slavery to the "principalities and powers" (Colossians 2:15; Ephesians 1:21–23). The ancient world was oppressed with the idea of fate, of individuals controlled by forces beyond their power. If modern men and women do not share the belief that destinies are directed by the stars or by supernatural beings, they are just as oppressed by the sense of being "pushed around", pawns in some cosmic game. It would seem that the Christian Church takes seriously this experience of fatedness (*e.g.* Romans 7:13-end) without losing its hold on a belief in the fundamental human ability to choose the good. Moreover it insists that, just as Christ sets us free from our deliberately chosen sinfulness, so too he sets us free from that evil which impinges on us and holds us back from entering into the glorious liberty of the children of God. God "disarmed the principalities and powers and made a public example of them, triumphing over them in (Christ)" (Colossians 2:15).

Pope John Paul struggles to reconcile this insight with his passionately held belief in individual human responsibility. It is "not out of place to speak of 'structures of sin' " and he insists that:

> It is important to note . . . that a world which is divided into blocs, sustained by rigid ideologies, and in which instead of interdependence and solidarity different forms of imperialism hold sway, can only be a world subject to structures of sin. The sum total of the negative factors working against a true awareness of the universal common good . . . gives the impression of creating, in persons and institutions, an obstacle which is difficult to overcome. [27]

Although such "social sin" is "the result of the accumulation and concentration of many personal sins"[28] without such a concept "one cannot easily gain a profound understanding of the reality that confronts us unless we give a name to the root of the evils which afflicts us." Yet the moral dimension cannot be lost. Confronted by such structures which go beyond personal sins we cannot escape the fact that "the real responsibility . . . lies with individuals. A situation – or likewise an institution, a structure, society itself – is not in itself the subject of moral acts. Hence a situation cannot in itself be good or bad."[29] It is "many sins which lead to 'structures of sin' " and "to diagnose the evil in this way is to identify . . . the path to be followed to overcome it."[30]

Such an emphasis on the inescapableness of personal decisions and personal responsibility, brings morality right back into the centre of the making of political judgements.

There can be no surrender to the impersonal "principalities and powers" whether of the class struggle or market forces. However this might by itself be open to misunderstanding. The deduction could be made that, if we were to get people right, policies which would serve the common good would automatically follow. As we often hear in evangelical circles: twice-born Christians will produce twice-born policies. But this, of course, is simply not true. Some very good and godly men have been disastrous rulers. Moreover I wonder whether one can safely say, without some qualification, that "a situation cannot in itself be good or bad". One would venture to think that the situation in Nazi Germany, Stalinist Russia, the Cambodia of Pol Pot and in racist South Africa could and ought to be described as "bad". In making this description one is certainly not absolving individuals of their moral responsibility, but registering the experience of coming up against monstrous evil which seems to go beyond the sum total of individual sins and which seems to carry individuals along, as by some demonic force. After all, the Apocalypse does not hesitate to designate the oppressive imperial might of Rome as the Beast.

The tensions and loose ends of a developing tradition – how far to go in politics

There is also a certain ambivalence in the Pope's teaching about the relationship of the Church to political programmes and activity. Of course there is a necessary ambivalence which is quite central to Christian faith for: "The Church well knows that no temporal achievement is to be identified with the Kingdom of God, but that all such achievements simply reflect and in a sense anticipate the glory of the Kingdom."

It is important to see clearly the balance of the Pope's teaching at this point, Some, who rightly say that no party political programme can be equated with the manifesto of the Kingdom, go on to dig a total gulf between the affairs of the city of Man and those of the city of God. This would make the teaching of the Church apolitical, totally irrelevant to the world of politics. Some, of course, would have it so. It has become part of the orthodoxy of the evangelical right that the Church is in business to convert sinners and promote personal righteousness but not to allow the Kingdom of God to impinge upon the political affairs of the kingdoms of this world.

Pope John Paul, following faithfully the teaching of Vatican II, will have nothing of such dualism:

> However imperfect and temporary are all the things that can and ought to be done through the combined efforts of everyone and through divine grace, at a given moment of history, in order to make people's lives "more human", nothing will be lost or will have been in vain. This is the teaching of the Second Vatican Council. . . ."When we have spread on earth the fruits of our nature and our enterprise — human dignity, fraternal communion, and freedom — according to the command of the Lord and in his Spirit, we will find them once again, cleansed this time from the stain of sin, illumined and transfigured when Christ presents to his Father an eternal and universal kingdom. . . . here on earth that kingdom is already present in mystery."[31]

Although we cannot speak of the political task as "building the Kingdom", yet it can be a fashioning of the bricks with which the city of God is built. What we do here and now on this earth has an eternal value and significance. There ought to be no escape from this tension which the gospel creates between the gospel and politics, for it is a highly creative tension; by it we are rescued from any idolatry of party manifestos, yet through it we are committed to the divine seriousness of our political actions. Grasp this ambivalence and we are equipped to be, what the city of Man cries out that we be, bent on working for human dignity, fraternity and freedom, and yet always perpetual critics of every programme which tries to move us in this direction.

Pope John Paul is quite clear about the necessity and dignity of the political task. Not only, as we have seen, does he pay a well-deserved tribute to the labours of politicians but consistently calls on Catholic laypersons to exercise their "royal priesthood" in the affairs of the city of Man. However he equally insists that the Church, as such, does not offer technical solutions to the world's problems: ". . . the Church does not propose economic and political systems or programmes, nor does she show preference for one or the other, provided that human dignity is properly respected and promoted . . . "[32]

And yet the difficulty of maintaining this distinction between the Christian vision which is to be applied to the secular world and the mechanics of this application is amply illustrated in the Encyclical. Already right-wing Catholics in the USA have demurred at the Pope's evenhanded criticism of marxist collectivism and western liberal capitalism. The Pope is similarly firm in his denunciation of economic mechanisms which operate against the good of Third World countries and explicit in his commendation of democratic forms of government which allow the free participation of the people. If the shape of the vision is to be sharp enough to capture the minds and imagination of a particular generation, then the borderline between the moral imperative and its practical realization is bound to become blurred. Here is the dilemma: Keep the message deliberately vague and safely clear from the political and it may just seem to float away on the winds but get into the intricacies of real problems and you may find yourself rapidly becoming pink or blue. In truth it cannot be said that, either in Franco's Spain or in present-day Poland, the official Church has been able, for good or ill, to steer quite clear of politics and there are situations, such as in South Africa, where studied neutrality is quite simply an option for the *status quo*.

The city of man and the city of God — A distinction to be maintained

This lack of clarity at the borders does not mean that the Church ought not to continue to struggle to maintain the distinction between the city of man and the city of God, for it remains essential that, while properly involved in the situation and committed to the cause of justice, she does not allow herself to be identified with any political regime. The very effectiveness of her distinctive involvement and commitment depends on the struggle to keep this proper distance, for, where the Church becomes identified with one political party, experience suggests she loses her cutting edge. What I suggest we have to do is, while being quite honest and open about the difficulty of maintaining this distinction, to be quite determined not to evade the difficulty by the sort of flight from politics which pretends to a higher piety but which is in fact an evasion of the human task.

Pope John Paul's social teaching has a claim on our attention because it presents a vision of society in which the importance of individual persons is reconciled with that of the common good. It is a coherent vision. It is consciously a contribution to a continuing tradition of thought and, instead of being tagged onto the bread and butter of Christian living as an extra luxury, is related and grows out of what is central to faith. It captures the mind and imagination, I suggest, precisely because in the relation between gospel and politics, the Pope chooses to skate on thin ice, to risk blurring this borderline by being specific, because he knows that above all "the Word" must be made "flesh", for the Christian there can be no escaping into dreams. To this point we must now turn as we ask how in a pluralist society this Christian vision can be effective.

Notes

1. *Redemptor Hominis* 14.
2. *Sollicitudo Rei Socialis* 1.
3. *Ibid.* 3.
4. *Gaudium et Spes* 3, quoted *Soc. Rei* 7.
5. *Gaudium et Spes* 1.
6. *Soc. Rei* 26.
7. *Ibid.* 27
8. *Ibid.* 35.
9. *Redemptor Hominis* 16.
10. *Ibid.* 1.
11. *Ibid.* 8.
12. *Ibid.* 20.
13. *Soc. Rei* 14.
14. *Soc. Rei* 15.
15. *Ibid.* 32.
16. *Redemptor Hominis* 14.
17. *Soc. Rei* 16.
18. *Ibid.* 19.
19. *Ibid.* 38.
20. *Ibid.* 39.
21. *Ibid.* 33.
22. *Ibid.* 39.
23. *Gaudium et Spes* 69.
24. *Summa Theol.* PtII–II Question 66 Articles 2 and 7.
25. *Gaudium et Spes* 32.
26. *Soc. Rei* 40.
27. *Gaudium et Spes* 36.
28. *Reconciliatio et Paenitentia* 16.
29. *Ibid.* 16.
30. *Ibid.* 37.
31. *Ibid.* 48.
32. *Ibid.* 41.

SIX

BECOMING MORE THAN A DREAM

The question is now whether these Christian convictions about humanity, the uniqueness of the individual and the need to share a common life, are to remain but dreams on the margin of society. A recent television programme on the way of life of the Free Presbyterian Church in the Hebrides posed this question poignantly. Here was an austere believing community going against the grain of modern culture, under siege fighting the encroachment of ferries on the Sabbath and the lure of pubs and cinemas. Despite its insistence on drawing lines on what seem rather trivial issues, there was a nobility about the attempt at such a distinctive life and, with its lovely Gaelic psalms, a cultural tradition without which the world would be the poorer. And yet was it not doomed to destruction? Were not the maggots of secularism already eating into its life as the faithful found themselves pondering on whether, while the pub remained forbidden, a wee dram at home was all right, or whether a film watched on television was as sinful as the same film watched in the cinema? A Catholic, despite the violence of this community's anti-Catholic prejudices, could not help taking his hat off to such rugged defiant conviction.

To withdraw or to dilute?

But that could just be an extreme example of the way faith in general is going, banished to the fringe, fighting an ultimately losing battle against the way of the world. It might continue for a long time to provide an alternative life-style for a minority but it would not contribute to society as a whole. Such communities might be of interest to anthropologists and even to the public at large, but as a subject for a television documentary with a David Attenborough explaining to us the significance of the strange goings on of this fast disappearing species. Indeed when we have to explain our convictions to outsiders, do we Christians not even now feel like such exotic though irrelevant relics by-passed by the onward sweep of modernity?

The temptation is, at this stage, either to modify our vision and allow ourselves to be swept along, buying the appearance of relevance at the cost of some trimming, or to snatch our vision away from the world, withdraw from the city of man, and hug it to ourselves in the wilderness. But our very convictions will allow neither dilution of the message nor withdrawal from the public scene. However crazy it may seem to those outside, we believe we are on to the truth, a truth which is not some theoretical luxury, but about that very reality with which those who wish to live "in the real world" have to come to terms. Our claim is not to some esoteric message to be enjoyed by a mystical minority which goes in for that sort of thing, but to what is essential for all human beings who want to find genuine fulfilment. Far from being peculiar to members of the club, this is for the world. It is this conviction which gives passion and urgency to the Christian mission. Far from hunting for scalps or engaging in imperialist conquests, we are trying to get a hearing for truth, for truth which people need as much as they need food, drink and shelter. Certainly Christians will get nowhere if they blunt the edge of this and settle for the quieter life of offering just another "way of looking at things" designed for "insiders".

A *pluralist society* – *the way things are*

The problem is easy to state – how to get a hearing for faith in its full rounded integrity – how our vision can capture minds and hearts with such force that action follows and things are changed. Our starting point in the West has to be the recognition that the pluralist society is a fact of life. By this pluralism I simply mean that we live in societies which are no longer dominated by a single vision of life, by a unified and coherent system of values. Instead we live in a supermarket in which beliefs and values compete for our attention. Although Christians, Moslems, Hindus and Jews are present in this society, none of their respective "visions" controls our life or is even held out to us as *the* authoritative ideal to be aimed at. Moreover men and women of religion have to recognize the presence and equal rights of atheists and agnostics. So the state tries to be the neutral state, holding the ring and allowing individuals, as far as possible, to cherish their own beliefs and live out their own freely chosen life-styles. Sometimes this is very difficult, as when Sikh motor cyclists want to wear turbans and not safety helmets, or some religion wishes to be faithful to dietary rules which involve the slaughtering of animals in ways which seem to offend laws against cruelty to animals. Neutrality is not always possible, but the "liberal" state in a pluralist society aims for such neutrality, tries to make as much space for the greatest number in a way which does not involve conflict or the destruction of a bare minimum of common life.

Neo-establishmentarianism – *the denial of pluralism*

There are of course some who deny that such a pluralism reigns in this country. They will say that Great Britain remains officially a Christian country. The sovereign is crowned in the setting of Christian liturgy, Parliament begins its proceedings with daily prayer, some bishops of the

Church of England sit by right in the House of Lords. Although these may be dismissed as formal vestiges of a past non-pluralist society, the upholders of this view reply that, on the contrary, these outward signs, admittedly small in themselves, yet point to an underlying and often submerged Christianity in the nation. Although Christian churches are not packed to the doors every Sunday, individuals turn to Christian faith at important stages in their lives, notably to celebrate marriage, the birth of children and death. Indeed there can be significant moments of corporate joy or grief when the community as a whole turns again to Christianity. The ending of the Falklands War was one such occasion, the communal grieving of Liverpool after the Hillsborough disaster another. What signs and symbols there are of common faith and values tend to be Christian and so force us seriously to modify the description of Britain as a "pluralist" society. Such are the views of what I would call "moderate establishmentarians". They would not argue that, because the "outward signs" of such allegedly underlying Christianity in England are controlled by the Church of England such faith should be treated as narrowly Anglican. They do not claim that the Englishman has a deep-down frustrated passion for the 39 Articles of Religion. Rather, they are ecumenically minded and would see the privileged position of the Church of England as a service offered to all Christians. In response you will find many Freechurch people saying that they would regret the disestablishment of the Church of England and many Roman Catholics who value the presence of Anglican bishops in the House of Lords.

Christianity as badge of national identity

But, of course, in a multi-racial society one has to ask how ecumenical such a model of Christian establishment can be? Does this take sufficiently seriously the presence and claims of very active faith amongst non-Christians? In recent years this has become an increasingly hot issue in education. We

116

have seen some tightening up on the part of the state of the content of religious education and school assemblies – a tightening which could be interpreted as a re-affirmation of the special place of Christianity. This has the predictable result of sharpening Moslem cries for special schools. "If the religion taught by the state is Christian, we claim the right for our children to be taught in the faith of Islam." So far this claim is resisted. That is not surprising, as Christian education in this context seems to be being used as a way of modifying the cultural identity of ethnic groupings. Such groupings are lectured to by Government ministers on the need to be assimilated and conformed to the British way of life.

This is understandable, as the state which wishes to develop a multi-racial society has to weave a careful path between allowing cultural variety to flourish and insisting that all its citizens live and behave as its citizens. The unacceptable face of separate cultural identity was revealed in the Salmon Rushdie affair, when some Moslems seemed to be responding to laws and values which were in conflict with those of this nation. This, of course, was a very revealing episode for it showed, not only that Islam possessed distinctive values, but also that liberal pluralist Britain possessed more common values than it had imagined! For a moment it gathered itself together and spoke with some passion about the precious freedom of writers to have their works published. But what is equally significant, when forced to declare our values, to nail our colours to the mast, we did so to a principle which owed more to the Age of Reason than to historic Christianity. When it comes to book burning, one has sadly to admit that historic Christianity has more often been on the side of the burners.

A mixed brew of values

It seems to be the case that what real common values and beliefs we now possess are a brew of many cultural influences. If sometimes we seem to touch upon a Christian nerve when confronted by the mysteries of life and death, at other times we touch a rationalist nerve which would bid us modify the passions and fanaticism of pure religion. One of the problems of reading history as a slow decline from "ages of faith" into comfortable disbelief or agnosticism, is that we consistently underestimate a quiet, hardly advertised, tradition of cynical secularism which has remained steadily present throughout. In other words, in the ages of faith there was probably more unbelief than we like to think. Our guess would therefore be that a new influx of cultural variety will in time enrich the brew of national common life. Beliefs and values strange to us are much like those foreign dishes at which initially we sniff with suspicion. Given time, of course, we are all eating those curries and discovering how convenient the Chinese take-away is. Christians have to be careful not to allow their own faith to be used as the equivalent of British fish and chips – the thing we cling to in the restaurant when the menu seems too exotic and frightening. The gospel will not allow itself to be used as a breakwater of British cultural identity against the incoming tide of foreign culture.

The value of pluralism

Moreover we have to ask whether, in terms of Christian faith, the opposite of the liberal plural society is really more attractive. Religious "establishments" abroad are nothing like so nice as at home. It all depends who is part of the "establishment"! Nor does the shadow of the "Ayatollahism" of the Christian right contending with American pluralism inspire much enthusiasm. Its modest successes should certainly alert us to the fact that any idea of inevitable progress in one "liberal" direction is simply false. But its main result – the revival of the death penalty and the ever-increasing queue of those waiting the attentions of the executioner – seems depressingly negative. In states where there is an established set of values, whether marxist,

118

Moslem or Hindu, and Christians are in a minority, they are found arguing with some vigour for the neutral state, for basic human rights to believe, practise and share their faith. It is not unreasonable to suggest that where they are in a majority they might continue to do the same on behalf of other minorities. They would do this not out of religious indifference, but in fact to affirm a Christian value – the inescapable duty of the individual to follow conscience and conviction. In so far as the state strives for neutrality and is strong enough to accept an ever-growing variety, it seems to be espousing a cause which Christians can embrace with some enthusiasm.

However the point I wish to make here is the simple one that the starting point for any advance into effectiveness must be the recognition that, whatever the symbols of religious establishment may imply, the fact of the matter is that we live in a society of competing values and beliefs, what I have called the "supermarket society". This, as the late Karl Rahner used to say, is a "must" not an "ought", *i.e.* while we must take things as we find them, we are not meant to have some ideological commitment to pluralism as the final truth about society. While we accept that it stands for certain values important for Christian maturity – the centrality of personal choice as against being dragged to conform to custom and convention – we are careful not to claim too much; for later we shall want to insist that this supermarket cannot be our goal, our resting place, that we have, again in Rahner's words, to "edge beyond" such pluralism.

Here though it is enough, against all the nostalgias which would imagine that there was some direct route back into European Christendom, to insist that "pluralism" is just a fact of life, a starting point, a reality with which we must come to terms. If Christians want to win their way with the vision which grips them, they have to win it in the open market and cannot any longer rely on a comfortable underlying assumption that "this is the British way". To my mind what is wrong, and indeed positively mischievous, about the symbols of "establishment" is that they insulate religious people from this reality and wrap them in the pretence that beneath the surface the English are Christian, and C. of E. Christian to boot, at heart. Scratch the Englishman and you will find his natural language is a blend of the King James Bible, the *Book of Common Prayer* and *Hymns Ancient and Modern*. The truth is in fact otherwise.

Communication and conviction

In the highly competitive supermarket the manufacturer, if he is to sell successfully, must look to the quality of his goods. This is not simply a matter of packaging because, although you can with careful advertising fool some of the public some of the time, you cannot do it all the time. Any body which sets out to communicate its values and beliefs must be a community of conviction. Political parties which are uncertain about their policies do not win elections. Thus the first task of Christians is to "be" the Church, establishing the credibility and coherence of its gospel by the way it lives it in the specific community of faith. If we possess insights into the value of the person and the need for human interdependence which are anchored deep in the fundamentals of faith, this is the way we have to live. However much it may be against the grain of contemporary society, we cannot avoid being non-conformists, aliens in a foreign land, those committed to a counter-culture. If cries go up that this is the way of "sectarianism", then quietly we shall have to bear this accusation and go on our way rejoicing.

The creative conviction of nonconformists

All social pioneers who break new ground are in this way sectarians, for at the end of the day it is not the conformists and the trimmers who have creative achievements to their name, but those of deep conviction who have been willing to stand against the tide. Creative artists only communicate through such stubborn conviction. They may endure isolation and much loneliness from an unheeding public and that will be painful because it is their longing to share their vision. But they will not compromise it and one day people will hear and see. It is the same with those who have laboured so bravely to alert us to the fragility of our world and to the inescapability of environmental issues. "The Greens" have been mocked, but now politicians vie to show that all the old political blues and reds really shade into green. Small communities of conviction do have their victories, do make their way in the world. Christians above all should remember that the cultural impact of Christendom depended on the earlier obstinate commitment of the nonconforming Church of the martyrs. It is a moving and still mysterious story about how this tiny body moved from the margins of society right to its very centre.

So there is nothing sterile and merely "inward-looking" about the attention the Church pays to it internal life. The fostering and the living out of the vision is the *sine qua non* of advance and cultural creativity. Indeed one suspects that it is lack of proper attention to this task of sowing, watering and tending the community of faith which has weakened its influence. Of course this basic task of formation has to be the spring-board which propels us deep into the waters of the world but it is not wisdom to spend our time chopping up the spring-board for firewood. Some "advanced" Christians, especially those of middle age, forget that in their pioneering they are going out with the provisions of a Christian background. To them it may now seem that these provisions are, like ships' biscuits, rather dry and inedible and this may lead them to think that pioneers can in future live off the country without such provisions. The fruits of insight into society spring in fact from roots deep in the central themes of faith. If we think that we can have the fruits without the roots, then we are deceiving ourselves.

Nurturing the roots of faith

So I venture to think that the single most important task for a Church seeking to be effective in society is to ensure the cohesion and consistency of its life by attention to these roots of faith. So it matters how the liturgy is performed, how this common "work" of the People of God really does gather up the deeply personal praying of unique individuals, how our human concerns are shown to open out into the mystery and compassion of God. Liturgical production is far more than a neurotic attention to rubrics or a strained effort either nostalgically to return to some golden past or to become immediate and relevant. It is to ensure the very embodiment of our vision, its proper performance so that all life can become this performance. Here human fulfilment, the unique value of persons in solidarity, is discovered in our solidarity through Christ with God.

But on this Eucharistic foundation, where we find our humanity in God, has to be built the life of the community which expresses what is there celebrated. Receiving the sacramental Body of Christ means being built up into the Body of Christ which is the Church. So the sort of issues which face the Church cannot be dodged in a mood of mystical fastidiousness. Here are the materials closest to hand in which our obedience to the vision is tested. How the diversity of human giftedness can flourish and yet serve the common life – how local Churches can have a proper distinctive way of life while never stepping out of the interdependence of the universal Church – how authority can be the real authority of the conductor of the orchestra, bringing the best out of his instrumentalists without reducing them to silent fear. These are all the stuff of ecclesiastical debate and politics. They cannot be dismissed as boring internal affairs which distract us from the real business of engaging with the world, or as matters too earthy, unspiritual and sordid for those who would soar to the heights. They are of importance because they are all to do with building on that Eucharistic foundation, with the word of our vision being made flesh. Put at its simplest: if we cannot handle these issues of liberty and fraternity convincingly on our own patch then our effectiveness in the world is weakened. This is clearly the case. Harm is done to the claims of faith, when individual giftedness and insight becomes self-indulgently heedless of the common life, when people are crushed by the ecclesiastical machine, or when the exercise of authority seems to derive from the techniques of Stalinist Russia.

Charity beginning at home – the search for Christian unity

The central issue for the Christian articulation of its vision must be the search for unity amongst divided brothers and sisters. Disunity is a scandal. Whether this is always a scandal to those outside our ranks, I begin to wonder. Certainly when Christians, as in Ulster, are at each other's throats, then that is perceived as scandalous. Conflict and even competition between those alleged to be brothers and sisters in Christ clearly contradicts the gospel we preach. The world sees that and does not believe. However I have to say that I am not so sure that the "denominationalism" of Christians set up in separate houses, emphasizing different aspects of faith and offering different styles of worship, is really perceived as scandalous. I suspect that here "market forces" have had their influences, that people actually look to religion as consumers and thus expect a wide range of goods. "It is no bad thing", the argument runs, "that we have this supermarket of faith. It is better than the old corner-shop which may have been more cosy but offered a pathetically small range of goods. As a consumer I have more freedom where I am able to choose from a variety of Christian packages." This I guess is the more usual attitude now to what we call Christian disunity. Certainly the public does not want us to get into fighting one another, and we are rightly required to behave in a civilized and friendly fashion, but I detect little enthusiasm for what the media call "mergers". If Christian churches came together and merged their identities then, it is feared, we would not only lose something of the spice and variety of life, but also be deprived of the range of religious "choice".

Variety the spice of Christian life

It is instructive to notice how the characteristic "oddities" of differing Christian bodies are picked on with enthusiasm by outside commentators and any watering down of such differences is bewailed and criticized. The world of unbelief likes its Christian packages neat and distinctive – Catholic peasants telling their beads with a muttering priest in the far distance; Nonconformist shopkeepers with sweat pouring down their faces bellowing hymns in over-heated brick chapels; decent C. of E. gentlepersons dreaming amidst the smell of old hassocks and decayed volumes of *Hymns Ancient and Modern* against the background of Cranmerian liturgy.

That there should be a sensitivity to the variety of Christian ways of life, seems very important; as does an alertness to the potentially tyrannical nature of the great united Church. Would not all that was warm, fascinating, and distinctive get lost in an ecumenical mush which would probably be the worst of all worlds? There is a serious question here about how variety can be preserved in unity. Of course the variety we are talking about is much more than the variety which may be perceived by theologians. It concerns the very texture and "feel" of Church life. Theologians can handle and probe our respective spinning of words, but they cannot handle the smell of hassocks or the particular ethos of Nonconformist hymn-singing. And yet such threads go to bind together this or that special package of faith to which individuals are drawn. It is this package, and no other, which carries to me and articulates for me what faith is. What will happen to such fragile products when the ecclesiastical tycoons move in for a merger or take-over bid? It is significant that zeal for such mergers is greater in the larger bodies of Christendom than it is in the smaller ones, suggesting perhaps that ecclesiastical imperialism is not wholly dead.

The lure of the "higher" ecumenism

If the public is indifferent to what we used to call "organic unity", the destruction of denominational containers, and there is a proper question to be asked about the future of variety, especially minority variety, in what appears to be the imperial Church, there is also some Christian disdain for what can be called "mere ecclesiastical re-arrangement". Ecumenism, it is said, should summon us to the real issues of our world, to breaking down barriers between men and women, between races and cultures, to the achievement of justice and peace. In the light of what has to be done for human unity, the affairs of denominations seem a trivial distraction. Racism and sexism, not heresy and schism, are the real enemies to be overcome.

It is heady stuff, and I am in agreement with it to the extent of saying that our internal Christian search for unity must consciously take place in the context of this search for the wider unity of the human race. This is only to say of course, what Vatican II said, that the Church is called to be a "sign or sacrament of human unity". But then a sign , if it to say anything, has to be definite, it has to have shape and form. So the question remains: "What sort of sign can Christianity, divided up into denominations, be of human unity?" The higher and wider ecumenism needs to be served by the lowlier and more restricted ecumenism. Love for the human race must, for Christians, begin at home.

Workshop for human unity

Instead of treating this search for unity as a bore or, after a few set-backs and disappointments, a wild impossible dream, we need to understand it as the work-shop of our basic vision. Here we really are coming up against the immensely difficult task of handling diversity in unity. How can variety burgeon and flourish and yet become, not like the variety and burgeoning of "I am for Paul" and "I for Cephas" a source of division and strife, but a service of the common life, a source of mutual enrichment?

It is easy enough of course to have a common unified life of regimented robots, of those sealed in a state of immature dependence. It is easy enough to have separate boxes for differing religious temperaments. In the one you can treat the riches of faith as an ideological jack-boot kicking individuals into submission. In the other you can treat the New Testament as an à la carte menu of religious experience from which we can select according to taste – "I rather like St. John." – "St. Paul is my man." – and then go for the Christian "box" which best reflects your chosen style. Religions of imperialism or of the supermarket are both easy and have their attractions, and yet they evade the real human task. The one squashes out unique giftedness and freedom. The other parcels out giftedness and deprives us of the possibility of being stretched and challenged precisely by that style of life and faith which is not quite "us".

"All things are yours" – the vision of organic unity

The old vision of "organic unity", which looked away from religious groupings gathered around a particular insight to the more motley mob gathered at one altar, was based on the obstinate conviction that the full riches of Christ are for all, that to be a complete human being I need something more than what immediately appeals to me. That may be a mad wild dream involving chasing the impossible instead of consolidating the possible, but who has achieved anything in society without pressing up against the barriers of what is deemed "possible"? The abolition of slavery and child labour and the granting of votes for women have all, in their time, been deemed "impossible".

Moreover the vision of "organic unity" at least addresses the fundamental issues of liberty and fraternity. We want variety to flourish, but not in the separate boxes of apartheid, in parallel development. The pursuit of a multi-racial society is precisely the preservation of unique identity within the common life of the community. Our belief is that the multi-racial society, far from being a merely negative attempt to preserve peace an harmony, goes for the gold of a more complex and thus richer common life. Our work for unity amongst Christians has thus to be more that the containment of difficult variety, more than the imperial victory of one body, more than the cobbling together of a united front in face of an unbelieving world. It too, if it is to be relevant to the great human task of achieving justice and peace with freedom, has to go for gold.

The demands of organic unity

This task is of course much more demanding that the achievement of any federation of separate Churches. It is harder to set up home together than to remain just good friends talking over the garden fence. In particular it requires of those communities, like the Roman Catholic Church, which most stress the importance of the bonds of unity, to make it evident that such bonds create a "broad room", a space in which variety can flourish. This is an unnerving task for a huge universal, multi-cultural Church. Such variety can always seem to be a threat to the bonds of unity. But the task equally challenges the smaller communities which fear the loss of their distinctiveness. Will not the big fish embrace the minnow only to swallow him up? Enormous resources of trust and good-will are required on all sides. This, in the end, can only be generated from that central Christian conviction that it is the will of the Lord that his scattered people should be so gathered and that through the ingathering no fragment of his gifts need be lost. The conviction is not simply that God has provided the map which shows us the way to such unity but also that he is the life, the active Spirit of convergence, working away amongst us, often wrestling with our stubbornness, to move us along that way.

Consecration for the sake of the world

If our Christian vision of the value of persons in community is to be effective, there can be no dodging of the domestic task. Before we can hope to capture the imagination of others, we have first to paint the picture and the paints we use are more than verbal. The whole way of life of the Church — its worship and its ordering as much as its preaching and teaching — has to be the picture, the embodied vision. We can talk big about freedom, justice and brotherhood, we can easily rebuke the sins of politicians, but if our own little world displays an absence of care for the individual, denials of freedom and justice and a "go-it-alone" rejection of unity, we shall be rightly told: "Physician, heal thyself." The Word, which we believe to be God's word, will not be made flesh.

And yet this domestic task is for the sake of the world and not for the construction of a comfortable holy huddle. Our distinctive way of life is quite simply believed to be the way of life for all humanity. This means that our identity has to be an inclusive not exclusive identity; that the city, however carefully protected with walls, has to have its gates open. In our search for effectiveness, we shall be looking for connections with a world which is not just a place of darkness but still, however scarred by sin, the work of a Creator who has pronounced his product "very good". In Christian terms — the "image" of this God in our common humanity, if defaced, is not destroyed. This means there is an eye in which the hook of the gospel fits, that we should expect what we say to "ring bells" where there is no explicit Christian faith.

SEVEN

SHARING IN THE SEARCH FOR CONSENSUS

Our concern for the internal domestic task of Christians does not absolve us from engagement with the world outside. The painting of our vision in the flesh and blood of the community of faith is not enough, for this community knows that it only finds authentic identity through risking it. We live by the fundamental law of the gospel which is: "whoever will save his life shall lose it; but whoever shall lose his life for my sake and the gospel's the same shall save it" (Mark 8:35). The church is born from the Cross; as St. John puts it, from the wounded side of the Saviour from which pours out the water of Baptism and the blood of the Eucharist (John 19:34). We thus find our true Christian identity at Calvary where the very identity of God is established, his glory seen, in the act of risking that identity in failure and the darkness of death. So Christian openness to the world and the obligation to share in tasks of the human city, do not follow from some compromise or accommodation with the secular but from the very heart of faithfulness. It is the gospel which forbids withdrawal to bask in the luxury of a religious ghetto.

There is a common human task to be engaged in, a task in which Christians have to abandon the lust to dominate and learn the more delicate skills of dialogue and co-operation. This mode of operation is clearly necessary from all we have said about the reality of the pluralist society. Our partners will be those of many religions and of none. But again it is faith and not compromising indifference which will lead us forward. The Word who is made flesh in Jesus does not come as some alien thrust into a godless world. He comes, says St. John, to "his own home", the light which shines in him is the same light which continues to flicker throughout the world (John 1:1–14). The hook of the divine fits into the eye of humanity which remains, though marred by sin, made in his image and likeness. Christians, instead of tip-toeing fearfully from the realm of light into the darkness, can go out confidently to seek the traces of God in a world which for all its denials and confusion remains his. We go in the expectation that God's word will ring bells, find a point of entrance in all men and women.

The pluralist society's crisis of confidence

There are particular reasons why we should be optimistic about getting a hearing in our age. There are signs that this liberal pluralist society is going through something of a crisis of confidence. The Salmon Rushdie affair was a symptom of this. Our Western liberalism with its too easily assumed freedoms was suddenly confronted by a fierce and intolerant form of Islam which challenged these assumptions. Liberals who had been to the forefront of welcoming a multi-racial, multi-cultural world – the more goods we have in the supermarket the better – found they had taken on board more than they had bargained for. Did their tolerance stretch to those who challenge such tolerance, whose conviction it is that the publication of *The Satanic Verses* constitutes an intolerable blasphemy? This was not just one critical opinion of a novel among many. It was a fierce condemnation of what was perceived as sin, backed with the threat of death to the unhappy novelist.

Liberalism appeared alarmingly defenceless. Those who had traded in cool scepticism saw the need for passionate conviction. Those who had been critical of the simple certainties of religious believers, holding that, in this life, there was no certainty to be found, became possessed of certainty and firmly nailed their colours to the mast. The burning of *The Satanic Verses* was seen as something like an act of sacrilege. With evangelical zeal "the right to publish" was proclaimed. The supermarket picture, it seemed, would no longer quite do. It was not enough to gather together more and more variety from which the individual was free to pick and choose. The supermarket to stay in business required the muscle of conviction, the confidence to draw lines, to say that some behaviour simply was not permitted.

The problem is that the liberal supermarket has no longer a common language in which to express and ground these necessary convictions. Embracing pluralism as the final good, variety the spice of life, gives Western society a babel-like quality. In two remarkable books; *After Virtue*[1] and *Whose Justice? Which Rationality?*[2] Alisdair Macintyre has explored this problem and has begun to edge in a direction in which solutions seem possible. "The most striking feature", he writes, "of contemporary moral utterance is that so much of it is used to express disagreements; and the most striking feature of the debates in which these disagreements are expressed is their interminable character. I do not mean by this just that such debates go on and on — although they do — but also that they apparently can find no terminus. There seems to be no rational way of securing moral agreement in our culture."[3] The only way, he argues, in which the urgent questions put to us are answered are in particular traditions of thinking. There seems no detached vantage point floating above these traditions. "We have learned that we cannot ask and answer those questions from a standpoint external to all tradition, that the resources of adequate rationality are made available to us only in and through traditions."[4] The way ahead, Macintyre seems to suggest, is through inhabiting and critically developing one such particular tradition. By "tradition" Macintyre means, not some old world relic, but as a stream of life wending its way through history, an active handing on of a coherent way of thinking which, though conscious of its continuity with and loyalty to a particular past, is able to attend to new questions and thus able to be a living developing tradition. Of course this leaves the thousand dollar question: Which tradition shall we inhabit and on what grounds do we decide to inhabit it?

The search for the common good

All of which brings us back to the point where we started, the need to advance beyond the supermarket view of an endless variety of personal options to some recognition of the "common life" and the "common good". A merely atomistic view of society with the neutral state holding the ring for this "do-it-yourself" activity simply builds Babel, leaving us unable to explain why we have chosen this liberal society. I wrote in an earlier chapter of how in recent years we have seen a determined assault on "consensus politics". While acknowledging that "consensus" always needs to be critically probed, it is surely an asset that cannot lightly be thrown away for at least it bears witness to a continuing sense of "the common good". In this country we have seen divisions opening up, the rich getting richer and the poor relatively poorer, an obviously visible concentration of wealth in the South East with an equally visible concentration of deprivation in inner cities and the North. In response to this there has been a new burgeoning of Welsh and Scottish nationalism. This is not surprising for when people feel shut out from the ongoing life of the nation, when they feel that there is not "one nation" but many, it is difficult to talk convincingly about "common values". Is it plausible that the values of the affluent South East should be the same as those of the North East? As the market prises open what remains of a common culture, we look for cultural roots nearer to hand and accordingly treasure whatever gives shape and coherence to life.

The continuing lure of consensus

There are signs that the abrasive market-led assault on consensus does not enjoy the support of the majority of the electorate. Opinion polls suggest that while many feel that the Thatcherite medicine was necessary to stir us out of a lethargic dependency, there is a good deal of anxiety about the individualistic values which it has generated and the social fragmentation which has inevitable followed. There seems to be a greater feel for "society" as a reality and for "the common good" than the new Conservatives have been willing to grant. Yes personal freedom to flourish is welcomed, but when it comes to issues of health, social welfare and education, people prefer money to be spent on these rather than returned in tax cuts. Perhaps we have underestimated a continuing tradition of social concern. What people call "the post-war consensus" – those common goals and assumptions on which political parties were generally agreed despite disagreement on the means to these ends – seems to have survived the assaults of Thatcherism.

Although the SDP/Liberal Alliance has collapsed into sectarian political infighting, the people who supported it in great numbers were, I suspect, casting their vote for a critical development of this consensus. The British have not been much addicted to polarized politics, to doctrines of class warfare or the confrontational mode of the new Conservatives. They suspect, rightly, that a great number of politicians from all parties agree on more matters than they care publicly to admit, and that this is unsurprising in view of that fact that outside pressures placed on any government render practical options somewhat limited. Any party's room to manoeuvre is far less than party propaganda leads us to believe. This fact of political life is perceived by the electorate so that an election battle looks, as they say, "just a game", an elaborate liturgical performance to convince us that we have more dramatic choices to make than are really present. In other words I judge that the British have a natural and somewhat shrewd affection for consensus or, as a critic would say, a taste for "fudge and mudge". This suggests that we would take quite happily to proportional representation and the coalition governments which would naturally follow. The electorate would see this as reflecting the large area of agreement which already exists between what it judges to be the more congenial politicians of all parties and as being in more accord with the "real world".

What I am suggesting is that the times are again propitious for consensus. The recent abrasive outbursts of "conviction politics" may have been necessary to poke the post-war consensus out of its rather cosy rut. We have had to ask ourselves: "In what direction do we want to go?" And that, as Tawney claimed, is a necessary question. But after ten years of Thatcherism the answer to the question does not seem to be in terms of unbridled individualism. Is it not something like this?

We have seen the dangers of a dependency society. We know that every bit of individual giftedness and effort is required, but we do not believe that this giftedness and effort is simply to be poured into the pursuit of private goals. We want a Britain in which all its citizens feel they belong. We believe in society. We believe that we must articulate and pursue a common good which is something more than the personal charitableness of those enriched by devotion to market forces. Public spending is not everything but in spending the taxpayers' money governments reveal what the electorate has decided to be priorities. We are not convinced that welfare, education and health spending should be any less a priority than defence or law and order.

Traditions of the common good and their development

Serious questions raised by the need to defend our liberal pluralist society and a continuing hankering after consensus by the electorate suggest that there is a job to be done in developing a vision of society which is something more that the free-for-all supermarket. I use the word "developing" advisedly, as I do not think that this is a case of starting from scratch. I would argue that there is an existing British "tradition" of the common good, with an emphasis on freedom and neighbourliness which has been assaulted, but not overcome, by the new market-orientated conservatism. Something of this tradition, with its particular values, was articulated in Richard Hoggart's classic *The Uses of Literacy*[5] and in his more recent autobiographical *A Local Habitation.*[6] Its influence on one stream of political life can be traced in Kenneth Morgan's *Labour People.*[7] My guess is that were a similar study to be done of the values of the old Shires Tory "one nation" culture or of continuing Liberal Nonconformist culture, a similar affirmation of individual liberty and social responsibility would be discovered.

I suspect that one reason for the present failure of the new "middle" liberal social democratic parties is precisely their newness, their lack of roots, that they do not clearly build upon the values and loyalties of a particular tradition. While the old Liberal Party could claim to be the traditional radical party of some parts of Great Britain, what are somewhat dismissively called the "Celtic fringe", the SDP was clearly starting from scratch, the brain-child of foot-loose middle-class radicals. Of course fundamentalism or nostalgic "traditionalism" will not do; if any tradition is to live it must change and develop. The travail of the Labour Party in recent years has been to come to terms with this fact. But it seems to be the case that new ground is most successfully broken by a party which can call on resources of traditional loyalty.

Making the Christian contribution in a pluralist society

Norman Dennis and A.H. Halsey in their *English Ethical Socialism*[8] give due weight to Christian influence in the development of this tradition on the left of British politics. It would be a mistake however to imagine that there can be some simple appeal back to Christian roots. This tradition is a brew, a blend of many influences, from which marxism and other forms of secular humanism cannot be excluded. It has been, as the saying goes, a Broad Church. This openness to many influences, the proven ability to take on board a number of value systems, will continue to be of the greatest importance in our multiracial society. But in the task of developing and refurbishing this consensus, whether on the political left, right or middle, Christians have an assured historic right to play a part. There is no need for us to be timid or apologetic.

We shall have to do this according to the rules of a pluralist society. It is no good either sitting around dreaming of some past model of Christendom or of bullying our way like the Moral Majority into positions of power where we can try to impose our way of life. If we are to be influential it can only be by reason and persuasiveness. The same must be true of other similar communities of conviction which will contribute to this new brew of consensus. This tradition has suffered more than enough from the muscle boys of the Militant Tendency and of market-force dogma. Theirs are not paths Christians should choose to go down.

Consistency – the witness of Christian humanism

The call is to participate in the reconstruction of consensus, to help articulate a view of the common good in which human freedom and human solidarity are reconciled. I suggest that in this exercise Christians will be found less banging the drum or laying down the divine law and more working for the consistency of a shared vision and the laying bare of the foundations on which that vision is based.

Christians will work for consistency by insisting on the seamless nature of our pro-life movement, that if we are really working for a humane society, designed for the fulfilment of individual persons this must include all persons. A belief in human equality rests on that respect for life which treats all with reverence. Here we can show that our opposition to pornography and sexual permissiveness springs, not from some arbitrary divine edict or a distaste and fear of human sexuality, but precisely from the denial of personal value and worth in such deviations. We want sex to be used for personal fulfilment, not persons for sexual fulfilment. Inconsistency in the abortion issue and over the rights of the disabled needs to be probed. A society which strives to be liberal and humane does not achieve this by giving rights to anyone over the life or death of anyone else. To treat the foetus as if it were just a disposable part of a woman's body and not at least a potential person is to offend against the insights of our vision. There is no more blatant inconsistency to be found than in the sight of feminist groups who have, with every justice, campaigned for women to be treated as persons, heaping abuse on those who campaign for the rights of those who are even more vulnerable than they are.

Digging to the foundation

If Christians can contribute to the development of consensus by the coherence of their pro-life vision, they can also do so by helping in the search for foundations on which the common good is built. Theologians, said the nineteenth-century Anglican F.D. Maurice, are less builders than diggers. Their task, he claimed, was to dig down through human values and aspirations and lay bare the foundation of them which is in nothing less than God. In recent years soggy consensus has been opposed by tough "conviction politics". The suggestion is that while consensus is an ivory tower of idle dreams brought to earth in compromise and muddle, "conviction politics" is a sinewy warrior well suited to the real world of the market place. If we are to achieve an effective consensus about the common good then it will have to acquire the muscle of conviction. Here those who have opted in the supermarket for the values of human freedom and solidarity often find themselves wrong-footed. Why these values and not others? What makes us believe that personal giftedness must serve the common good? Why do we reject the market as the measure of all things? We need answers to these questions which go rather further than proclaiming them as our chosen options, our personal preferences.

Applying the mind

To be committed to the values of freedom and solidarity is a matter of far more seriousness than the choice of this hat rather than that, this brand of dog food rather than that. The trouble is that many ordinary people have come to conclude that moral choice is based on just this sort of irrational option. We need the sort of reflection about our values which will show that such choices are reasonable. Now, of course, moral philosophers spend a good deal of time and energy in such pursuits, but too often their reflection is treated as the hobby of an elite. Indeed the terrifying fact is that just when we most need to foster and popularize the reflective clear-thinking skills of philosophy, government policy in higher education considers such study most disposable. Man cannot live by business-studies alone. Instead of orientating education towards industry and the acquiring of vocational skills, we need to be spreading precisely this ability to ponder and think critically. In other words education is for human fulfilment and flourishing and not to provide fodder for industry.

Capturing the imagination

Not that reflection, by itself, will move us into convinced action. If education cannot be measured by the market, neither can politics really endure the "philosopher king". Both minds and imaginations need to be fired if we are to achieve "conviction consensus". This perhaps is the secret of the strange once universal appeal of marxism. What on paper looks a very turgid teutonic ideological analysis becomes flesh in a passionate moral crusade. The very idealism which Marx himself rejected in favour of "scientific" socialism, has in fact been the fuel which has driven the crusade which marches under his banner. While the doctrine of Surplus Value held as little excitement as the doctrine of Double Predestination, the cry of "Workers of the world, unite!" had something of the power to move of the evangelical "Repent and be saved!". Christians can understand this, being themselves in the business of both reflecting and stirring the heart. They know that conviction must capture both mind and imagination. Part of their role in the development of the new consensus will be to aid this marriage of reasonable reflection to passionate conviction. This in itself will make great demands on the community of faith, which has tended in recent years to allow this marriage to come apart. Warm eager devotion has floated free of its intellectual anchorage so that it has sometimes seemed that in religion one has to be either silly or arid.

Communities of conviction – threat or necessity

Participation in this reconstruction of consensus alongside those of many faiths and those of none is the task for Christians in a pluralist society. But this does not mean that the Church loses its nature as a community of conviction. There is a real problem raised by such communities in a pluralist society. Can they really play by the rules, for are they not, with their arrogant claims to possess final truth,

139

by nature intolerant? Such, as we have seen, was the nature of the clash between sections of Islam and liberal Western society over *The Satanic Verses*. While we patted ourselves on the backs for a tolerant society which contained Moslems as well as Christians, what were we to do when our very tolerance was turned on by the tolerated? Indeed, with the resurgence of fundamentalism of all sorts throughout the world, communities of such burning conviction constitute a real threat to a mild liberalism which thought all that sort of thing had passed away. A liberal society could take such communities as exotic species of pets to be treasured, but when they became ravening rottweilers, then it was a different matter.

Another fascinating incident in 1989 brought us up against a community of conviction. The Lord Chancellor, Lord Mackay, was suspended from membership in the Free Presbyterian Church. His offence was that he had attended a Roman Catholic Requiem Mass for a friend and colleague. As this little Church considers the Mass to be a blasphemy and the Pope to be "anti-Christ", the Chancellor's act of friendship was held to be sinful. Such bizarre beliefs were thought by most Christians to be either shocking or laughable. And yet did we not all, a Roman Catholic included, have a sneaking admiration for a rugged sect which had no respect for the person of the Lord Chancellor?

Lord Rees Mogg in the *Independent* revealed the serious side of this ambivalence. "The Lord Chancellor", he wrote, "is an admirable character, one of the best men in public life." But this Lord Chancellor is the product of a life-long devotion to and membership of this tiny sect. How, asked Lord Rees Mogg "is a good man produced and his personality shaped by so defective a Church?" A rugged intolerant sect produces the goods. We, who like Lord Rees Mogg, call ourselves, and are proud to call ourselves, liberals need to attend to his unusually self-critical liberal questioning. We may shudder at the bizarre beliefs of the Free Presbyterian Church, we may loathe its intolerance and yet do we have "the power to form consciences"? "At what step along the road to religious liberalism do we lose the vital ability of religion to form personal character and stability?"

Our society, it seems, needs its communities of strong conviction. It needs the rock of rugged faith to make its pluralism strong enough to go on being open. While such communities have the ability to erode the free liberal society, indeed to fuel the very darkest conflicts and wars which stain our world, they have also the ability to enrich us with the conviction we most need. A very serious responsibility is thus laid on these communities. If they lose the salt of their identity they will have nothing to offer the world, but if they treat this salt as a privileged possession, the spice of superiority, they will fill the world with poison. The way to make rugged faith creative rather than destructive is not by compromise or watering down, but by entering into that faith more deeply. By doing this believers acquire the secure conviction which makes them relax. Deep secure faith rescues us from anxious preservation of the barricade and spurs us boldly to throw open the city gates.

The search for consensus and loyalty to particular traditions

So far I have spoken about the Christian calling to participate in the edging beyond the pluralism of the supermarket towards some vision of the common good, the development of a new consensus. I hope that I have not ironed out the variety of traditions which will have to flow into this brew. While I believe that there are convictions about personal freedom and human solidarity which we have in common and which we need to articulate in common, it must be recognized that we edge towards this goal from different religious and political commitments. I do not see that this advance involves a weakening of such commitments. Our task will be to inhabit our traditions and to develop them in the conviction that there are already values which we share in common and in the hope that our separate lines of tradition are capable of sufficient convergence to reconstruct a common life. Although in politics we should be much more relaxed about coalitions and alliances between parties, this should not mean the destruction of the identity of parties. It is these traditions which foster loyalty and passionate conviction through their particularity. How dull elections would be without these distinct colours! It is of course the same with religions. The growth of genuine dialogue and friendship between adherents of different religions does not come by way of some artificial syncretism, but by the exploration of our distinct traditions in a spirit of openness and willingness to learn from the other. However my assumption is that rooted in different political and religious faiths, we are capable of advancing towards some agreement, some beliefs about the humane society which we can share with reasonableness and passion. The maintenance of artificial differences and the denial of areas of agreement is not just perverse but a demonstration of a lack of secure conviction. To bolster sagging identity we feel the need to accentuate our difference, our uniqueness.

On not evading the political task

Of course such a search for consensus goes beyond the purely political. We have been talking about the participation of Christians in the search for common goals, for some agreement about the common good. But this does not mean that the more narrowly political task can be dodged. The advance beyond dependency and independency cultures to the more mature culture of interdependency will not be achieved without the nuts and bolts of political arrangement. As I have said before by "politics" I mean simply the ways and means whereby we order the affairs of the human city. Christians who desire particular ends cannot neglect the means to those ends. Because human beings disagree about ways and means there arise in democratic societies political parties. Christian involvement in the political life of a country like ours will inevitably mean party political involvement – at least to the extent of casting our vote at an election for one party or another. Political seriousness means that we cannot float above what people rather disparagingly call "mere party politics".

The Church in politics

There is immense nervousness about the idea of the Church in politics. It suggest either highly placed ecclesiastics telling the simple faithful to vote for some, normally right-wing, party or agitating radical priests squashing the gospel within a marxist framework. Let us be clear, to talk about the Church in politics is not to talk about priests or bishops in the first place. In order for the Church to "be" somewhere, you do not need to have a whole lot of clergymen. The Church is fully present in the person of its laywomen and men. Indeed this is the Church of the *diaspora*, the Church scattered in the world, not the Church gathered for worship and prayer but it is the "Church of Christ" all the same. The continuing identification of "the Church" with its ministerial priests has to be overcome. While the latter are properly concerned with the articulation of faith in word and sacrament, the laity are concerned with the no less important task of being the anonymous, unlabelled presence of Christ in the secular. Indeed the laity, as salt and leaven, are a deeper presence than that of ministerial priests. In their anonymity and secular expertise, making their way not by ecclesiastical status, but by involvement in the world, theirs is the way of Christian effectiveness and authority in such situations. Priests, bishops and popes can only be the servants, the resource men of such front-line troops. This really does have to be grasped if we are to get this issue, the relationship of Church to politics, right. The royal priesthood of the laity has the right to tell the ministerial priesthood how it should be served.

The role of the laity and the role of priests

Ideally one would say that here the laity are the "front-line" and priests are the supply men. Ideally we should recognize that deep, and therefore necessarily anonymous, penetration into the secular is a lay task, while priests serve in the order of signs, announcing, and making explicit the reign of Christ. However it does not always work out like this. There are situations in which the articulation of the gospel requires that political responsibility be highlighted and in which ministerial priests have to act as pioneers. The fact that such situations are not typical, in that the normal political "grey" of ambiguity has here given way to a clearer position in which at least Christians can say "It is not right to pursue that path", does not mean they are unusual. We have in fact seen the Church taking sides, in and through the involvement of bishops and priests, in many situations in recent years. Not only have most Christians ruled out the support of apartheid in South Africa, or the exploitation of the political far right, with its death squads, in South America; but also the Catholic Church in general, with Pope John Paul II in particular, has had no little influence in the spectacular challenge of Solidarity to Polish Communism. It seems that, in order to make the Christian call to political involvement clear in certain situations, the ministerial priesthood has to take the risk of leading from the front.

The fact that this happens, as it has often happened in the history of the Church, and that it is right that this should happen, should not blur its anomalous nature. The anomaly of priests and bishops leading where laity should lead is something to do with the "clericalization" of the Church and the failure to see that on the front-line of the Church's mission, it is for the laity to speak with the authority of deeper involvement and for the clergy to serve this mission. What the Christian community needs above all in these days is to gather those who are willy nilly involved in political tasks and get them reflecting on these tasks. They would need the service of bishops, priests and theologians, but it is they the laity who should be dictating the agenda for it is they who have the secular expertise.

Christian detachment – the perspective of the Kingdom

What has to be made clear is both the whole-hearted involvement of the Church in the political task and yet its refusal to bow the knee to political ideologies. In this commitment which falls short of absolute loyalty to the "party", lies the particular contribution which Christians make to political life. All parties when they achieve power become lazy, complacent and lacking in self-criticism. It is one of the problems of "one-party" rule, that it lacks the necessary needle of opposition. It is to this fact of the inertia of party loyalty that the Communist bloc is having to attend. In a less dramatic form it is to be met in local government where one party has ruled for years without effective opposition. Christians refuse the idolatry of the party programme. However good the manifesto is, it is not the manifesto of the Kingdom of God. Always a gulf lies between the rule of God and rule of this world.

The restless critics

This does not mean that we are to acquiesce in some dualism between the two kingdoms as if God's rule had nothing to do with our rule, as if we had no obligation to move our ordering of society in the direction of the divine ordering. God's rule remains in judgement on ours and it is the Christian task precisely to edge policy nearer the divine. This means there can be no "settling down", no sense of the task completed. Christians should thus act as agents of discontent in the political system. It is part of their involvement to be for ever pushing at the boundaries of the politically possible. We should go on aiming high and daring what others do not dare. Political advance requires a continual challenge of the "possible". Politics needs men and women of muscle ready to move mountains.

The sober realists

But this does not make the Christian contribution to politics one of wild "idealism". We are not to be amongst those who are only happy in the purity of the wilderness far away from the ambiguities of power. Just because the party manifesto is not held to be the manifesto of the Kingdom, we are freed for the necessary, and properly political, task of pushing our society just a few steps in the proper direction. While we shall be wildly ambitious about our goal, we shall be capable of being very modest and realistic about those hesitating advances in this direction. At the end of the day we shall have preferred to travel a little way in reality than a long way in our minds. Christians will not be by nature enemies of "political compromise". Politics can be accepted as "the art of the possible", provided that it is seen within the context of the wild impossibilities of God's Kingdom.

Christian participation in politics means participation in party politics. Here the Church will only nail its colours to the mast of one party in the direst of circumstances. "Christian" parties like "government by the saints" have an unhappy history. To be deplored are all dogmatisms which could claim that no honest disciple of Christ can be either a Tory or a Socialist. At least in this country we have the good fortune of being able to be loyal, and therefore critical, members of all main parties.

Critical party membership

Believers will have particular contributions to make in differing parties. On the political right, they will want to explore the fullness of the notion of freedom, and seek to move it on from the mere ability to choose from a well stocked supermarket. They will be wary of "market mysticism", treating market forces with such deference that it borders on idolatry. Believing that the "market" is an apparatus which will serves human freedom, they will insist that it is made for humanity and not humanity for it. While wishing to affirm the reality of individual responsibility as against the tendency to sink back into a dependency culture, Christians of the right will want to revive that sense of social responsibility which belonged to the "one nation" school of conservatism. They will see such responsibility as something more than encouraging "the rich man in his castle" to consider "the poor man at his gate".

On the political left, the Christian contribution will also be marked by a critical loyalty. Here it is the "mysticism of the class struggle" which is to be challenged, an idolatry of the forces of history which are believed to work for the good of the classless society. While there is much marxist analysis from which we can still learn, in particular the constant reminder that our ideas and ideals do not float above history but come to us with the soil of particular social and economic conditions clinging to them, we have to resist the power of marxism to become an all-embracing framework. Marx can be a good servant but a bad master.

The notion of equality will have to be rescued from the dreariness of sameness. The left has to learn to foster giftedness and allow variety to flourish. Our belief in equality precisely entails the freedom of each person to become all that he or she is capable of becoming. Christians can assist the left to see the values of equality and freedom reconciled in fraternity or solidarity. The social dimension of human existence, the fact of the Human Arch which makes us look beyond independence to interdependence, must make us look critically at the ways in which the left has understood the embodiment of solidarity. There can be no swift move from the rejection of individualism to the espousal of state centralism and the nationalization of the means of production. Certainly there are some forms of "social

147

ownership" which seem to require a large measure of state control. It is difficult to see the argument for allowing natural monopolies, such as water, gas and electricity, in which there can be no measure of genuine competition, to become private monopolies. However, there are all sorts of ways in which justice can be done to our social nature which fall below the social organ of the state.

Catholic social teaching in its principle of "subsidiarity" recognizes and seeks encouragement for those social forms which are less than state forms. The healthy society, it insists, is one in which families, schools, universities, trade unions, professional associations, local and regional government should be allowed to flourish with a proper autonomy. In fact it is in these lesser, more intimate, social groupings that we first realize that we are more than isolated atoms. One of the more sinister legacies of the new conservatism has in fact been the destruction or weakening of the independence of such groupings – particularly the unions, local government, and education. The left, if it can acquire the courage to be more critical of its passion for central state control, has the opportunity to espouse the cause of such "subsidiarity", thus making more evident the bond between personal freedom and human solidarity.

An alternative Christian vision

I hope that I have made it clear that I see the possibility of the developing of different political traditions. The image of the Human Arch, pointing beyond dependence and independence to interdependence, could give us all a shared vision of the common good but would allow continuing political debate about the ways to achieve this end. I suggest that this approach neither deifies nor dodges the political task.

A somewhat more abrasive approach is argued by Professor Brian Griffiths in his book *Morality and the Market Place*.[9] Professor Griffiths speaks from the political

Right. Indeed, as Head of the Prime Minister's Policy Unit at 10 Downing Street, he could be said to speak from the very heart of the Thatcherite revolution. He also speaks as a committed evangelical Christian who, far from allowing his faith to be detached from his political commitment, believes that it fuels and fires it.

Professor Griffiths is an advocate of the market economy because it is a wealth creator of proven ability. However, not only does he see this economy threatened by the marxist left, but also undermined by the libertarian right. Writers like Milton Friedman and Friedrich Hayek who make freedom an absolute, have in fact created the "crisis of capitalism". Indeed both socialism and libertarianism are seen as the twin and malign offspring of secular humanism.

> The sickness or crisis of capitalism is not at heart a technical matter but a lack of legitimacy with respect to the system itself. . . . For the market economy to work, the society of which it is part needs to believe in certain kinds of values: it must lay great store by individual responsibility and also have a non-egalitarian view of what constitutes social justice.

What philosophy can then undergird the market economy and make it acceptable? Like the American cavalry it is Christianity which comes to the rescue. "Christianity can provide such values and has indeed done so during the period of industrialization throughout much of the Western world". [10]

What strikes the reader is the firmness with which Professor Griffiths attaches Christianity to the market economy. The necessary tension between the insights of faith and all political arrangements is relaxed. No legitimate political pluralism is envisaged and the conflict between the forces of light to the right and those of darkness to the left is dramatically polarized. By a process of caricature all socialism is tarred with the brush of atheist Marxism and secular humanism. There is not a mention of those Christian

149

influences on British socialism, of the likes of Tawney and Temple. The Professor is fiercely critical of liberation theology, which he accuses of fitting faith into a marxist framework, but what he does not perceive is that he himself is busy fitting Christianity into the framework of the market economy. In seeing faith as legitimizing capitalism, not only providing it with an acceptable face, but fuelling it with precisely the values it needs, Griffiths provides the almost perfect example of religion as the sanction for the *status quo*, and thus confirmation of the marxist critique of religion.

If no political pluralism is envisaged neither is any religious pluralism. The Brandt report is taken to task for its statement: "We take it for granted that all cultures deserve equal respect, protection and promotion." No, cries the Professor . . . "they do not. Cultures express values which shape institutions and motivate people – some of which as we have seen promote wealth and justice and liberty and others of which do not."[11] All this talk about pluralism is held to be "thoroughly humanist". Yet when Griffiths bids the Church take up with greater zeal the task of evangelism, we are left wondering whether this is really for the sake of immortal souls or for the sake of fashioning those values which will create wealth. Are missionaries really the agents of the gospel or of capitalism? There are moments when the Professor comes near to suggesting that the answer must be "both" for amongst the fruit of the spirit must be counted not only love, joy and peace but the more abrasive values of the market economy as well.

However *Morality and the Market Place* is a book to be read, not only because it author is well-placed to influence the course of Conservative thinking, but because he clearly articulates an evangelical right-wing social gospel of growing importance. Professor Griffiths' contribution should assist the debate amongst Christians and spur us on to tease out our theological differences. His position is that "Jesus was not a social reformer with a social message who produced a blueprint for society".[12] The Kingdom which he announces is "relevant to personal ethics. It is also the basis for the life of the Church."[13] Moreover "in calling people to follow him" material matters are put "in their true perspective".[14] If the Gospel of the Kingdom is not of immediate relevance to the ordering of society, a careful following of the text of the Old Testament is. Here Professor Griffiths finds quite detailed and practical guidance. Many theologians, he claims, make deductions from the Bible "so general (and sometimes even vague) that it is of little practical help in choosing between the main alternatives of the world today".[15] Not so his reading of Scripture. Seven sturdy pillars are erected which, including a "positive mandate to create wealth", the affirmation that "private property rather than state, social or collective ownership is the Christian norm for society", that "each family should have a permanent stake in economic life", that "the relief and elimination of poverty rather than the pursuit of economic equality should be a Christian concern", certainly make a sure foundation for the Thatcherite revolution.

The debate which is called for in the Christian community must centre on whether this concentration on the Biblical text [16], which of course turns out to be a concentration on selected texts, is the correct theological approach. Is such particular political guidance to be mined from the Old Testament? Is the teaching of the New Testament to be reduced to providing a spiritual perspective? In my judgement Professor Griffiths gets too much detail out of the former and in practice renders the latter irrelevant to the problems of society. My approach has been a more doctrinal one which, I would insist, is not thereby less biblical. I have wanted to ask the Christian community which has pondered down the ages and continues to ponder on Scripture: "What is the nature of our humanity created in the image and likeness of God, defaced by sin and yet renewed in the living, dying and rising of the Lord Jesus?" That is, "What is it to be a fulfilled human being living in a real world?" I have concluded that we are made and redeemed for freedom and fellowship – indeed that the heart of our liberty is to be free for one another in love. We are to be built into the Human Arch of interdependence. While Professor Griffiths offers a highly detailed legitimation of the market economy, I offer a guiding image, a clear enough goal, leaving the inescapable task of politics, the steps towards that goal, to the wit and wisdom of fallible human beings. That Professor Griffiths and I come to rather different conclusions is partly due to the fact that we are operating with rather different theologies. What this indicates is that, for all our proper Christian zeal for action and service, there remains a continuing task of theological reflection and debate. *Morality and the Market-Place* will help to stimulate this.

Notes

1. Duckworth 1981.
2. Duckworth 1988.
3. *After Virtue*, p. 6.
4. *Whose Justice, Which Rationality?*, p. 369.
5. Chatto and Windus 1957.
6. Chatto and Windus 1988.
7. Oxford University Press 1987.
8. Clarendon Press 1988.
9. Hodder and Stoughton 1982, ²1989.
10. *Morality and the Market Place*, pp. 40–41.
11. *Ibid.* pp. 148–9.
12. *Ibid.* p. 87.
13. *Ibid.* p.10.
14. *Ibid.* p. 87.
15. *Ibid.* p. 91.
16. *Ibid.* p. 76.

EPILOGUE

UNCERTAIN
TRAVELLERS

The travellers seem to have reached one of those points when
it is no good simply plodding on. That way risks going
energetically in the wrong direction. We need again to ask
where we want to go and then to discover paths which may
get us there.

In the months I have been writing this book I have detected
a declining assurance that British society is moving in the
right direction. The Thatcher revolution seemed to have
brought such a lovely sense of simple certainty. We knew
that we ought to head away from the maternal embrace of
the all-intrusive state to individual liberty and responsibility.
New-born as home and share owners, we were eager for
yet more opportunities to make our way further up the
ladder of individual achievement. But then something made
us look down from our solitary perch. We saw those who
had not made it; the homeless huddled in the doorways of
shops or under bridges, the unemployed who would never
again have their work valued, the single-parent families, the
mentally sick ejected from hospitals into those communities
which the market economy had so carefully dismembered,
and the shivering elderly for whom a government minister
could find no better advice than the exhortation to knit
woolly hats. All these we discovered were not aliens from
some other planet but humans, of our own flesh and blood.

"Ah", they say, "now you have done so well out of our
opportunity society, you will be willing, of your bounty,

to give to these beggars. Let the face of our successful capitalism be made acceptable by the gracious smile of charity." And there was no word about justice, no recognition that we were members one of another, so that these our flesh and blood had a right to a fair share of the good things of this world. And there was no such word because we had come to believe that "society" was a superstition, that there was no such thing as the "common good". My neighbour and I were just lone individuals scrabbling up our privatized ladders. All talk about "common values", even Victorian values, was so much windy rhetoric in this real world in which the market snapped the fragile bonds of community and prised us apart.

Such were the simple certainties of the eighties. We turn now into the new decade with such certainties shaken. We are less sure that this is the way to human fulfilment. Once more the fog has moved in and the travellers pore over maps and guide-books in search of the way ahead. Even in those heartlands of dogmatic certainty, at the political conferences in the autumn of 1989, breezes of questioning could be felt stirring amidst the stale breath of Party faith and loyalty.

This book has suggested that Christians have a contribution to make to this questioning and searching. Of course we are not in possession of some guide-books of unchallenged authority. Perhaps we can only persuade our fellow travellers that we have something to say through our experience as long-seasoned hikers. Our community has travelled this terrain before. Time and again we have had to squeeze our way between the rocks of individual freedom and those of the common good. We can roll up our sleeves and show many a scar as evidence that we are no strangers to such conflicts. But we do have an image to guide our travels. It is that of the Human Arch. Beyond the lonely ladders this is what we see, human interdependence which is more than both the immature dependence which saps responsibility and more than the adolescent independence which would condemn us to solitariness. Our fulfilment as free persons lies in the freedom to lean upon one another, to give and receive love. This is no pretty "social" flourish which some Christians add to the bread and butter business of sacrament and prayer. It springs, I have claimed, from the very centre and substance of faith.

Of course Christians are not the only travellers looking for the way ahead. We live in a pluralist society, a supermarket of values and beliefs, in which the search for some shared goal often seems well-nigh impossible. Yet there is no way ahead except by renouncing the attempt to dominate the discussion, except by joining as equal partners in discovering a common vision of the good life for the city of humanity. This does not mean capitulating to the ideology of pluralism or accepting that society can do nothing more than create conditions for the maximum number of individuals to pursue their private goals. Pluralism is our starting point. It is just a plain fact that, on this mountain top, there are a number of highly articulate travellers all with strongly-held views as to where we should go next. But it is also a plain fact that the supermarket view of values is not enough to hold society together. If the band of travellers is to stay together and not simply disperse into an assortment of solo adventurers, each striking off alone, it has to work painfully towards a common mind.

I do not underestimate the complexity of this task. With the cold winds of secularism blowing round our ears, it is tempting to head for the nearest mountain hut there to enjoy the provisions one has so carefully preserved. For very understandable reasons Christians, like the adherents of other religions, are becoming increasingly preoccupied with preserving the integrity of the treasures of faith, building flood barriers against the encroaching waters of unbelief. I repeat, this reaction is understandable and indeed points to a task which from the times of the New Testament onwards has been a necessary one for the Church. There is nothing dishonourable about defending the faith. The world is not served by a pale diluted gospel. Yet we can only

defend the faith as God defended himself on Calvary –
through that generous love which goes on throwing its arms
around the world and through that ever deeper commitment
to humanity. It is through this "deep solidarity with the
human race"[1] in solidarity with the crucified one, that our
Christian identity is in fact established. There can be no fear
of loss of faith along this path into the concerns of the city
of man. For this is also the path into the joyful freedom and
interdependence of God himself.

Note

1. *Gaudium et Spes* 1.

Also available in Fount Paperbacks

The Sacrament of the Present Moment
JEAN-PIERRE DE CAUSSADE

'It is good to have this classic from the days of the Quietist tensions with its thesis that we can and must find God in the totality of our immediate situation . . .'

The Expository Times

The Poems of St John of the Cross
TRANSLATED BY ROY CAMPBELL

'Mr Campbell has recreated the extraordinary subtlety of the music of the original in an English verse worthy of it and that climbs from aspiration to ecstasy as if it were itself the poem.'

The Guardian

Thérèse of Lisieux
MICHAEL HOLLINGS

A superb portrait of one of the most popular of all saints.

'This book is well worth recommending . . . presents a simple factual outline of Thérèse's life and teaching . . . (with) incidents . . . applied to our own everyday lives.'

Review for Contemplatives of all Traditions

I, Francis
CARLO CARRETTO

This unusual and compelling book is a sustained meditation on the spirituality of St Francis of Assisi, bringing the meaning of his message to our time.

'A book one will not forget.'

Eric Doyle, The Tablet

Fount Paperbacks

Fount is one of the leading paperback publishers of religious books and below are some of its recent titles.

- ☐ FRIENDSHIP WITH GOD David Hope   £2.95
- ☐ THE DARK FACE OF REALITY Martin Israel   £2.95
- ☐ LIVING WITH CONTRADICTION Esther de Waal   £2.95
- ☐ FROM EAST TO WEST Brigid Marlin   £3.95
- ☐ GUIDE TO THE HERE AND HEREAFTER
  Lionel Blue/Jonathan Magonet   £4.50
- ☐ CHRISTIAN ENGLAND (1 Vol) David Edwards   £10.95
- ☐ MASTERING SADHANA Carlos Valles   £3.95
- ☐ THE GREAT GOD ROBBERY George Carey   £2.95
- ☐ CALLED TO ACTION Fran Beckett   £2.95
- ☐ TENSIONS Harry Williams   £2.50
- ☐ CONVERSION Malcolm Muggeridge   £2.95
- ☐ INVISIBLE NETWORK Frank Wright   £2.95
- ☐ THE DANCE OF LOVE Stephen Verney   £3.95
- ☐ THANK YOU, PADRE Joan Clifford   £2.50
- ☐ LIGHT AND LIFE Grazyna Sikorska   £2.95
- ☐ CELEBRATION Margaret Spufford   £2.95
- ☐ GOODNIGHT LORD Georgette Butcher   £2.95
- ☐ GROWING OLDER Una Kroll   £2.95

All Fount Paperbacks are available at your bookshop or newsagent, or they can be ordered by post from Fount Paperbacks, Cash Sales Department, G.P.O. Box 29, Douglas, Isle of Man. Please send purchase price plus 22p per book, maximum postage £3. Customers outside the UK send purchase price, plus 22p per book. Cheque, postal order or money order. No currency.

NAME (Block letters) _____

ADDRESS_____

_____

_____

While every effort is made to keep prices low, it is sometimes necessary to increase them at short notice. Fount Paperbacks reserve the right to show new retail prices on covers which may differ from those previously advertised in the text or elsewhere.